Emergency Response Planning In College Libraries

CLIP Note # 40

Compiled by

Marcia Thomas
Director of Technical Services
Illinois Wesleyan University
Bloomington, Illinois

Anke Voss
Director of Special Collections
Urbana Free Library
Urbana, Illinois

Edited by Marcia Thomas

College Library Information Packet Committee
College Libraries Section
Association of College and Research Libraries
A Division of the American Library Association
Chicago 2009

426389797

9-29-09

The paper used in this publication meets the minimum requirements of the American National Standard for Information Sciences-Permanence of Paper for Printed Library Materials, ANSI Z39.48-1992.

Library of Congress Cataloging-in-Publication Data

c.1

Emergency response planning in college libraries / compiled by Marcia Thomas, Anke Voss ; edited by Marcia Thomas.
    p. cm. -- (CLIP note ; #40)
  Includes bibliographical references.
  ISBN 978-0-8389-8524-3 (pbk. : alk. paper) 1. Academic libraries--Safety measures. 2. Academic libraries--Security measures. 3. Emergency management--Planning. 4. Library materials--Conservation and restoration--Planning. 5. Library surveys--United States. I. Thomas, Marcia L., 1950- II. Voss, Anke. III. Association of College and Research Libraries. College Library Information Packet Committee.
  Z679.7.E44 2009
  027.7028'9--dc22

2009027571

Printed in the United States of America.

13 12 11 10 09   5 4 3 2 1

Cover design by Jim Lange Design

TABLE OF CONTENTS

        Bucknell University
        Bertrand Library
        Lewisburg, Pennsylvania

        Washington and Lee University
        Washington and Lee University Library
        Lexington, Virginia

        University of Richmond
        University of Richmond Libraries
        Richmond, Virginia

        Trinity University
        Coates Library
        San Antonio, Texas

        Belhaven College
        Warren A. Hood Library
        Jackson, Mississippi

Belhaven College
Warren A. Hood Library
Jackson, Mississippi

Moravian College
Reeves Library
Bethlehem, Pennsylvania

Georgia Southwestern State University
James Earl Carter Library
Americus, Georgia

Bucknell University
Bertrand Library
Lewisburg, Pennsylvania

Wofford College
Sandor Teszler Library
Spartanburg, South Carolina

St. John's University
Alcuin Library
Collegeville, Minnesota

Elon University
Belk Library
Elon, North Carolina

Siena College
J. Spencer & Patricia Standish Library
Loudonville, New York

Jacksonville State University
Houston Cole Library
Jacksonville, Alabama

Wofford College
Sandor Teszler Library
Spartanburg, South Carolina

Siena College
J. Spencer & Patricia Standish Library
Loudonville, New York

St. John's University
Alcuin Library
Collegeville, Minnesota

Bucknell University
Bertrand Library
Lewisburg, Pennsylvania

Jacksonville State University
Houston Cole Library
Jacksonville, Alabama

Bucknell University
Bertrand Library
Lewisburg, Pennsylvania

Wofford College
Sandor Teszler Library
Spartanburg, South Carolina

Trinity University
Coates Library
San Antonio, Texas

St. John's University
Alcuin Library
Collegeville, Minnesota

Washington and Lee University
Washington and Lee University Library
Lexington, Virginia

Jacksonville State University
Houston Cole Library
Jacksonville, Alabama

CLIP Notes Committee

Amy J. Arnold (Chair)
East Tennessee State University
Sherrod Library
Johnson City, TN

Ms. Sharon M. Britton
Bowling Green State University,
Firelands Campus
Huron, OH

Jennie Elaine Callas
Randolph-Macon College
McGraw-Page Library
Ashland, VA

Rachel C. Crowley
Briar Cliff University
Sioux City, IA

Eleonora Dubicki
Monmouth University Library
West Long Branch, NJ

Lynda Duke
Illinois Wesleyan University
The Ames Library
Bloomington, IL

Janet S. Fore
Saint Mary's College
Cushwa-Leighton Library
Notre Dame, IN

Christopher Millson-Martula
Lynchburg College
Knight-Capron Library
Lynchburg, VA

Barbara Whitney Petruzzelli
Mount Saint Mary College
Newburgh, NY

Debra Cox Rollins
Louisiana State University At Alexandria
James C Bolton Library
Alexandria, LA

Ms. Kathryn K. Silberger
Marist College
James A Cannavino Library
Poughkeepsie, NY

Erin T. Smith
Westminster College
Mcgill Library
New Wilmington, PA

Doris Ann Sweet
Simmons College Library
Boston, MA

Nancy J. Weiner
William Paterson University
Wayne, NJ

Acknowledgements

The compilers would like to thank Amy Arnold for her willingness to revive this publication and Eleonora Dubicki for her editorial work and encouragement during the revision process. A special thank you is extended to David Jensen, former director of Van Wylen Library at Hope College, for initiating this publication and conducting the survey.

INTRODUCTION

INTRODUCTION

OBJECTIVE

The College Library Information Packet (CLIP) Notes publishing program, under the auspices of the College Libraries Section of the Association of College and Research Libraries, provides college and small university libraries with current documentation on relevant library practices and procedures. This *CLIP Note* provides information on disaster emergency response planning and management to assist librarians in the creation and updates of emergency response plans. Included are the results of a survey administered to college and university libraries that participate in the CLIP program and sample documents submitted by the libraries.

BACKGROUND

This College Library Information Packet updates *Emergency Planning and Management in College Libraries* by Susan C. George (1994, CLIP Note no. 17), now out of print. Many of the questions posed in the original survey were retained. After all, the risk of incurring a disaster has not changed substantially. However, our awareness certainly has. Events such as Hurricane Katrina and September 11 remind us that library buildings, collections, and staff are vulnerable to a frightening array of disasters. The compilers of this publication were curious about the effect that recent events might have on library emergency policies and plans. Certainly the development of campus-wide emergency response systems in the wake of the tragedies at Virginia Tech in 2007 and Northern Illinois University in 2008 point to the need for libraries to assess whether their plans and resources coordinate with those of the larger institution. Many colleges and universities now have their crisis management plans and manuals available online, as does Washington and Lee University's Emergency Management site at http://www.wlu.edu/x3000.xml.

Ideally, a disaster preparedness plan will address prevention, immediate emergency response, recovery and salvage procedures, and rehabilitation of damaged materials. Should development of a comprehensive plan seem overwhelming, SOLINET's website reminds us that "a 'phased' approach can also be applied to disaster preparedness….It is acceptable, as a first phase, to begin with a few sections (even in outline form), particularly if the institution focuses first on those issues that are of greatest concern" (Southeastern Library Network 2009). The bibliography contains a list of selected publications, available in print and on-line, that provide the library and archives professional with resources that are needed in planning for and responding to disasters in the library. These publications include both general guidelines and examples of specific procedures, including tools for writing your own disaster plan. The reader is advised to periodically review the professional literature, as research continually leads to new developments in the area of disaster preparedness.

Sample documents from emergency plans and policies in this publication, as well as online resources cited in the bibliography, can serve as templates for local adaptation. Acknowledging that events following Hurricane Katrina "unfold[ed] in unforeseen ways," Louisiana State

University's CIO Brian Voss asserted, "The best hope is to be prepared to handle a core set of events as best you can and to be aware that you will have to deal with surprises" (Voss 2006). While few of us will experience the wide-spread destruction wrought by hurricanes or acts of terrorism, many of us have faced or will experience smaller-scale emergencies at some point in our professional career. Now is the time to update an existing disaster plan or create a new one.

SURVEY PROCEDURE

The authors used standard CLIP procedures for administering the survey: the CLIP Note Committee reviewed and revised questionnaires before they were sent to a pool of small and midsized libraries that have agreed to respond to CLIP Notes surveys and submit sample documents for publication. This survey of the organization, planning, and level of disaster preparedness at college and small university libraries was conducted online in 2005, employing a program designed by Ryan McFall of the Computer Science Department at Hope College. The survey questions were adapted from the survey conducted by Susan C. George for the 1994 edition of this CLIP Note. Unfortunately only 68 replies to the survey (one of which was unusable) were received from the 221 libraries queried, yielding a disappointing 30% response rate.

Due to unusual circumstances, publication of the 2005 survey was put on hold. However, the current CLIP Notes Committee decided to proceed with the publication of the results of the survey, along with an up-to-date bibliography and current sample documents from respondents to the 2005 survey.

ORGANIZATION OF DOCUMENTS

Most of the plans and policies received from libraries and used in this publication were submitted whole. The compilers made the decision to separate whole plans and policies into sections, as best as possible, and arrange individual sections into categories according to content covered.

ANALYSIS OF SURVEY RESULTS

ANALYSIS OF SURVEY RESULTS

General Information on Survey Respondents (Questions 1-8)

These questions gathered general data about libraries responding to the survey. Libraries ranged in size from 78,443 to 2,200,000 volumes with a median of 294,738. They represented institutions ranging in size from 860 to 13,000 students with a median of 2,524. Total expenditures for materials ranged from $10,086 to $4,441,201 with a median of $550,630. Median FTE staff was 8.45, ranging from 1 to 24; median FTE support staff was 8.5, ranging from 1.5 to 50; and median for FTE student assistants was 9.15, ranging from .37 to 129. Of the 67 respondents, 75% were from private institutions and the remaining 25% percent from public colleges, with18 reporting branch libraries.

Past Experience with Emergencies and Disasters (Questions 9-13)

The purpose of this set of questions was to determine how many libraries had experienced emergencies, as well as gather information about those experiences. Fifty of the sixty-seven respondents (75%) had experienced an emergency of some sort, with several reporting multiple emergencies. The most frequently cited emergency involved water (61%), followed by weather (9%) and fire (8%). However, 20% of these respondents reported "Other" and when these responses are taken into account, results show that mold ties with fire as the third-most frequently reported emergency. Libraries also experienced noxious fumes, power outages, vandalism, earthquakes, hurricanes, defective sprinkler systems, tornados, repeated flooding, a chemical plant explosion a mile from campus, and medical emergencies. One library reported, "We have had all of the above. Some of the more unusual: chemical plant explosion within a mile of campus; air handler caused a flood in special collections; storm water back up in basement in special collections room." These examples serve notice to all of us that emergencies may come in many forms and when they are least expected. Libraries can react quickly and purposefully in the face of such situations if they have prepared for emergencies and have practiced their plan of action.

Thirty-six (71%) of the libraries that experienced an emergency had plans in place to deal with the event. Only one reported that the plan failed: "Disaster was so large, the disaster plan was overlooked by the administration." Another commented, "In instances where it did not work as well as planned there was confusion about who was in authority to direct emergency efforts." This demonstrates the importance and value of preparation and communication for coping with emergencies.

Emergency Response Planning: Manuals (Questions 14-26)

This set of questions was intended to determine which libraries had some type of emergency response manual, how the manuals were managed, and what information was included.

One in four of all libraries that responded to this survey did *not* have a manual to help provide direction to the staff in an emergency. It is abundantly clear that libraries with plans are better positioned to recover more quickly and with fewer losses than institutions without an emergency response plan.

Of the fifty of the libraries that reported having emergency response manuals, 59% had been updated within the preceding two years. Only thirteen (27%) of the plans were scheduled for annual revisions; thirty (61%) revised their plan "as needed." One library reported, "Library manual focuses on collection recovery, but references and is linked to campus-wide emergency response procedures, which are also updated annually." Revision as needed permits the manual to reflect changes in procedures, personnel, and facilities as they occur. An annual review in addition to a policy of "as needed" insures that the plan is kept up to date. Responsibility for revision appears to be divided among an emergency response team (31%), the library director (25%), a preservation officer (10%), or another librarian/individual (34%).

When asked about distribution of the manual, twenty-two (45%) of the forty-nine respondents distributed their manuals to all library staff and the campus safety officer and another ten (20%) distributed only to library staff. One library reported distributing their plan to the local fire department as well as the campus safety office. The remaining 32% reported a variety of distribution plans more inclusive than provided for on the survey. Some of the additional individuals included chief academic officers, heads of physical plant, and chief administrative officers. The importance of including the communications office or chief information officer (CIO) cannot be overstated, yet only one library mentioned distributing the manual to their CIO. At the time this publication went to press University of Richmond Libraries, Bertrand Library at Bucknell University, and Leyburn Library at Washington and Lee University had their plans accessible on their websites. Some libraries have produced flip charts for reference at public service desks and elsewhere.

Forty-nine (96%) of the fifty-one libraries with manuals reported that it covered emergencies dealing with water, fire and weather; thirty-four (67%) dealt with medical emergencies, accidents; twenty-six (51%) with bomb threats, terrorism, and hostages; thirty-seven (73%) with building structure, power failure, and environmental issues; twenty-six (51%) with theft, vandalism, or threatening persons. Surprisingly, less than half reported that their plans dealt with computer or electronic network failures. In response to a follow-up question on this topic (question 24), only thirteen of forty-nine respondents (27%), reported their manual included procedures for dealing with unplanned shut down and recovery of automated systems. Thirty-four (71%) included a list of collection priorities; however, collection priorities in manuals submitted by libraries for inclusion in this publication appear to be aimed at recovery from damage to print collections. Given the proportion of library budgets allocated to electronic resources and virtual collections, disaster response plans should pay particular attention to this area.

Another surprise: eleven of forty-nine respondents (22%) reported that their manual did not include an evacuation plan for staff and users. Evacuation plans for some libraries may be incorporated into a campus-wide plan, yet moving people away from a dangerous situation must have the highest priority, especially in a building as public as a library. Twenty-nine of forty-nine respondents (59%) claimed to rehearse their plan (most often a fire drill as part of an institution-wide procedure). One library had conducted a mock disaster.

Following an essential best practice, all forty-nine respondents who had a manual reported that theirs included a list of individuals to contact and/or a calling tree. More specific information on checklists is contained in the analysis of the following survey questions.

Emergency Response Management (Questions 27-60)

In addition to gathering specific information about emergency response manuals and plans, the authors wanted to know about management issues, such as who is in charge when disasters occur; how and to whom responsibilities are assigned, who provides training sessions and how frequently, what resources are available and where those resources are located.

Emergency Response Teams (Questions 27-35)

Forty-one of sixty-five respondents (63%) reported having a designated Emergency Response Team, although a total of forty-two respondents actually answered this set of questions. Many libraries had a different name for their team, which may account for the difference. One library reported, "Since we are a small staff, the entire staff on duty responds at the time of an emergency." Another noted, "Important distinction: we are not concerned with public safety activities such as bomb threats or disruptive patrons, only with threats to library materials." The size of the response teams ranged from two to more than eleven individuals, but most commonly numbered between two and seven. Almost half of the respondents reported that their library's team included the library director/dean. Examples of others on the team are: archivists, special collections librarians, department heads, circulation staff, computing services staff, preservation officers, conservators, other library administrators, maintenance staff, and head of physical plant. One of the larger libraries organized its Disaster Recovery Team into functional units consisting of a "Services Continuity Team, Communications Manager, and Salvage Team." Another had work teams for salvage, bibliographic control, and supplies. These institutions have thought carefully about what kind of organization is needed to recover from a disaster.

Team membership was most often determined by individual job responsibilities, staff who volunteered, or appointment by the library director. Ten of forty-one respondents (24%) reported team members from outside the library, while only one had a member from outside the institution. Teams from thirty-one of forty respondents reported to the library director/dean; others reported to an assistant library director, archivist or preservation officer. One team reported to the campus safety officer. Only 49% percent of the teams had a formal charge and only 26% met regularly.

Training (Questions 36-40)

Of the forty-one respondents who had emergency response teams at their library, only 60% reported that the *team* received training. More broadly, twenty-seven of sixty-four respondents (over 40%) reported that their libraries did not offer *any* training. The thirty-seven libraries that did offer training provided it to librarians (58%), support staff (56%), and/or students (30%). Question 37 serves as an important reminder that many libraries rely heavily on student staffing and thus should be informed of emergency procedures and receive relevant training. The most frequently cited types of training were preservation/resource recovery (59%) and fire extinguisher use (72%). Only 31% offered training in planning the management of emergencies – another important reminder that planning itself is an acquired skill and planning for emergencies is acquired knowledge.

As expected, a variety of individuals and groups sponsored and scheduled training, but most often from within the library (director, emergency response team, conservation / preservation officer, or other librarians and staff). Other participants included campus security / safety / physical plant, local and regional consortia, and community police and fire departments. One library paid for Red Cross training in first aid and CPR. Another reported that circulation staff provides training for student workers. At least one library uses videos to support in-person training.

Of the forty-three respondents reporting that their institutions offered training, only fourteen did so at a minimum of once a year. The remainder answered that they received infrequent and sporadic training. Thus with only 60% of all survey participants reporting that they had received any training at all, only one in five of all responding libraries could claim that their staff had received up-to-date training in any area of emergency response management.

Risk Assessment (Question 41)

Hazard analysis and risk assessment answer the question: "What would happen if a hazard event occurred in my library?" The process of quantifying the potential loss of life, personal injury, economic injury, and property damage provides a solid foundation for the rest of the emergency planning process. Of the sixty-five libraries responding to this question, twenty-seven (42%) reported having risk assessment offices at their institution. One commented, "The responsibility rests with the Director of Facilities and Maintenance, the VP for Business Affairs, and the Director of Campus Safety." Others mentioned specific offices on their campus, such as "Internal Control Officer" and "Safety Services." See also the analysis of question 56.

Checklists (Questions 42-54)

Sixty of sixty-five responding libraries (92%) have a checklist of people within the institution to contact when an emergency occurs. (As noted previously, all forty-nine respondents who had manuals reported that their manual included a list of individuals to contact and/or a calling tree.) Checklists included individuals in public safety (90%), physical plant (88%), emergency management (43%), business offices (40%) and food service 18%). Only 73% reported updating the checklist regularly.

Forty-four of sixty-four libraries (69%) reported having a checklist with locations of in-building emergency equipment, with thirty-six responding that the checklist was updated regularly and forty-three responding that the checklist was in an accessible location. Only twenty-six of sixty-three respondents (41%) indicated they had a checklist of on-campus emergency equipment, with twenty-three updating the list regularly. Thirty-eight of sixty-two libraries (61%) had a checklist of off-site emergency recovery suppliers and services, with twenty-seven updating.

Thirty-seven of sixty-five respondents (58%) reported having a checklist of outside consultants with expertise in specific types of emergencies, such as specialists at regional conservation centers.

Miscellaneous (Questions 55-59)

Sixty-one of sixty-four respondents (95%) reported regular inspection of library emergency equipment.

Only eight of sixty-two responding libraries (13%) had a written hazard analysis. See also the analysis of question 41.

Staff or emergency response team members from fifty of the sixty-five responding libraries (95%) knew the location of circuit breakers in their library, but staff from only 66% of those libraries had access to the circuit breakers.

Reports of emergency incidents are required in thirty-seven of sixty-five responding libraries (57%).

Self Assessment (Question 60)

How did 66 survey participants rate their ability to deal with a library disaster?
5 Excellent (8%)
34 Good (51%)
15 Fair (23%)
12 Minimal (18 %)

Conclusions

No library should be without a continually updated disaster response plan. Three-quarters of the responding libraries had experienced a disaster and three-quarters had some form of a written plan for emergency response and disaster recovery. One hopes that in the three years since the survey was administered, the other 25% have adopted a written plan. With many templates and models available online, it's easier than ever to adapt an existing plan to local circumstances.

Most of the plans reported were rooted in the library's print era. It appears that many libraries need to bring their plans up-to-date in regard to recovery from unplanned interruptions of electronic services. For example, one of the authors' libraries recently suffered a loss of service when its server was hacked from outside, causing a crash that brought down the whole integrated library system. Response plans and recovery procedures need to be in place to deal with these types of emergencies, in addition to flood, fire and water.

A few of the plans submitted indicated that copies were available in the librarian's office and perhaps with one other person. Any library employee with responsibilities for identifying, reporting, or responding to emergencies, as well as appropriate campus officers such as the head of the physical plant, should have access to a copy of the manual or checklist. In addition, anyone with responsibilities for managing responses should have a copy at home.

There seems to be a lack of training for libraries in *how* to plan for response to emergencies. Such planning might include hazard analysis, risk prevention and mitigation, methods of training, preparation of manuals and instructions, and organizing for response. More alarming is the statistic that only 54% of all survey participants reported that training of *any kind* was offered at their libraries.

BIBLIOGRAPHY

SELECTED BIBLIOGRAPHY

Websites

American Library Association. Disaster Preparedness and Recovery. <http://www.ala.org/ala/aboutala/offices/wo/woissues/disasterpreparedness/distrprep.cfm>
(accessed March 2, 2009). A general guide to seeking federal funding to aid in disaster response and recovery.

American Library Association. Disaster Response: A Selected Annotated Bibliography. ALA Library Fact Sheet 10. <http://www.ala.org/Template.cfm?Section=libraryfactsheet&Template=/ContentManagement/ContentDisplay.cfm&ContentID=25420> (accessed March 2, 2009). This fact sheet contains links to disaster preparedness web sites whose primary role is emergency response or conservation, and to information on available training, as well contains a select book bibliography.

Heritage Emergency National Task Force. <http://www.heritagepreservation.org/PROGRAMS/taskfer.htm> (accessed March 2, 2009). Provides preparedness and post-disaster information resources for library, archives, and museum collections and buildings.

MBK Consulting. Disaster Prevention & Emergency Planning. <http://www.mbkcons.com/wkshp/disaster/disasterfront.htm> (accessed March 2, 2009).
The company specializes in providing consulting and educational services to libraries, archives, historical societies, museums and other cultural institutions, and offers several popular workshops in disaster response planning. MBK Consulting was founded by Miriam Kahn, author of *Disaster Response and Planning for Libraries.*

The National Archives. Emergency Preparedness. <http://www.archives.gov/preservation/emergency-prep> (accessed March 2, 2009). Tools to provide sound introductory information to private individuals and public institutions in preparing for either small or large scale events.

National Institute of Health. NIH Listserv. Disaster Information Outreach by Librarians. <https://list.nih.gov/archives/disastr-outreach-lib.html> (accessed March 2, 2009). This listserv is a discussion forum for librarians, information specialists and anyone interested in responding to their community's needs for information services in support of disaster preparedness, mitigation, response and recovery.

Northeast Document Conservation Center and the Massachusetts Board of Library Commissioners. dPlan™: The Online Disaster-Planning Tool. <http://www.nedcc.org/services/disaster.dplan.php> (accessed March 2, 2009). NEDCC and the Massachusetts Board of Library Commissioners (MBLC) have created dPlan, a free online program to help institutions write comprehensive disaster plans. dPlan provides an easy-to-use template to develop a customized plan.

National Park Service. Museum Management Program. Conserve-O-Grams. <http://www.cr.nps.gov/museum/publications/conserveogram/cons_toc.html> (accessed March 2, 2009).

Short, focused leaflets about caring for museum objects, published in loose-leaf format. Topics covered are relevant to individuals who have collections of fine arts, furniture, ceramics and glass, leather work, books and papers.

ProText: Protecting and Preserving Collections. Archivists, Collectors and Museums. <http://www.protext.net> (accessed March 2, 2009). Disaster recovery supplies for librarians, archivists, collectors and museums.

The Regional Alliance for Preservation (RAP). <http://www.rap-arcc.org> (accessed March 2, 2009). Provides information and resources on preservation and conservation for cultural institutions and the public throughout the United States.

Resources for Conservation Professionals: Conservation OnLine. Disaster preparedness and response. <http://cool-palimpsest.stanford.edu/bytopic/disasters> (accessed March 2, 2009). CoOL, a project of the Preservation Department of Stanford University Libraries and Academic Information Resources, is a full text library of conservation information for libraries, archives and museums.

Southeastern Library Network (SOLINET). Disaster Resources. <http://www.solinet.net/preservation/preservation_templ.cfm?doc_id=71> (accessed March 2, 2009). A collection of publication and video lists, online leaflets, and internet resources.

Special Libraries Association. Disaster Planning Portal. <http://www.sla.org/content/resources/inforesour/sept11help/disip/index.cfm> (accessed March 2, 2009). Listing of selected articles, monographs, videos, and websites in the area of disaster planning.

Books and Articles

Alire, Camila, ed. 2000. Library Disaster Planning and Recovery Handbook. New York: Neal-Schuman Publishers, Inc.

Breighner, Mary, William Payton, and Jeanne M. Drews, eds. 2005. *The Risk and Insurance Management Manual for Libraries*. Chicago: Library Administration and Management Association.

Brooks, Constance. 1993. Disaster Preparedness. Washington, DC: Association of Research Libraries.

Cravey, Pamela. 2001. Protecting *Library Staff, Users, Collections, and Facilities: A How-To-Do-It Manual for Librarians*. New York: Neal-Schuman Publishers, Inc.

Drewes, Jeanne M., ed. 2005. Risk and Insurance Management Manual for Libraries. Chicago: American Library Association.

Drewes, Jeanne M. and Julie A. Page. 1997. *Promoting Preservation Awareness in Libraries: A Sourcebook*. Englewood, Colorado: Libraries Unlimited.

Field Guide to Emergency Response: A Vital Tool for Cultural Institutions. 2006. Washington, DC: Heritage Preservation.

Fortson, Judith. 1992. *Disaster Planning and Recovery: A How-To-Do-It Manual for Librarians and Archivists. How-to-do-it Manuals for Libraries no.11.* Ed. Bill Katz. New York: Neal-Schuman Publishers, Inc.

Halsted, Deborah D., Richard P. Jasper, and Felicia M. Little. 2005. *Disaster Planning: A How-to-Do-It Manual for Libraries.* New York: Neal-Schuman Publishers, Inc.

Kahn, Miriam. 2003. *Disaster Response and Planning for Libraries.* 2nd ed. Chicago: American Library Association.

----------------. 2004. *Protecting Your Library's Digital Sources: The Essential Guide to Planning and Preservation.* Chicago: American Library Association.

Patkus, Beth L. and Karen Motylewski. 2007. "Disaster Planning." *In Preservation of Library and Archival Material,* ed. Sherelyn Odgen. Andover, MA: Northeast Document Conservation Center. Also available at <http://www.nedcc.org/resources/leaflets/3Emergency_Management/03DisasterPlanning.php> (accessed March 2, 2009).

Voss, Brian D., "What Would Ozymandias Think about Disaster Planning?" *EDUCAUSE Review,* 41 (2006): 76–77.

Wellheiser, Johanna G. and Jude Scott. 2002. *An Ounce of Prevention: Integrated Disaster Planning for Archives, Libraries, and Record Centres.* 2nd ed. Lanham, Maryland: Scarecrow Press.

Wellheiser, Johanna G. and Nancy E. Gwinn. 2005. *Preparing for the Worst, Planning for the Best: Protecting Our Cultural Heritage from Disaster.* Proceedings of a Conference Sponsored by the IFLA Preservation and Conservation Section, the IFLA Core Activity for Preservation and Conservation, and the Council on Library and Information Resources, Inc., with the Akademie der Wissenschaften and the Staatsbibliothek zu Berlin, Berlin, Germany, July 30 - August 1. München: K.G. Saur.

SURVEY RESULTS

SURVEY RESULTS

Note: Direct quotes from survey participants are indicated in italic font. For most questions, only selected comments are included.

General Information Questions 1-8

1. Number of FTE students enrolled, fall 2004: **median=2,524; range=860-13,000 (67 responses)**

2. Number of FTE Librarians: **median= 8.45; range=1-24 (67 responses)**

3. Number of FTE Support staff: **median 8.5; range =1.5-50 (67 responses)**

4. Number of FTE student assistants (hours of student help per week during the academic year divided by 40): **median=9.15; range=.37-129 (62 responses)**

5. Number of physical volumes in all libraries on campus: **median=294,738; range=78,443-2,200,000 (66 responses)**

6. Number of library branches (including the main library): **median=1; range=1-6 (67 responses)**
   - 48 One branch
   - 8 Two branches
   - 4 Three branches
   - 4 Four branches
   - 2 Five branches
   - 1 Six branches

7. Total Expenditures for materials: **median=$550,630; range=$10,086-$4,441,201 (64 responses)**

8. Is your institution **(67 responses)**
   - 50 Private
   - 17 Public

Emergency Response Planning and Management Questions 9-13

9. Have any of your libraries experienced a disaster? (67 responses)
   - 50 (75%) Yes
   - 17 (25%) No (go to question 14)

10. What was the nature of the emergency? (51 responses)
    - 33 (64%) Water
    - 10 (20%) Other (see below)

5   (9%)   Weather
4   (8%)   Fire
1   (2%)   Medical

"Other" responses:
Mold (4)
Multiple events (3)
- *Most recently water, but medical, weather-related and noxious fumes from welding in the past*
- *Water, weather, vandalism, fire alarm (emergency averted), blackout*
- *We have had all of the above. Some of the more unusual: chemical plant explosion with a mile of campus; air handler caused a flood in special collections; storm water back up in basement in special collections room*

Earthquake (1)
Power outage (1)

11. At the time of the emergency did you have a response plan? (51 responses)
36 (71%) Yes
15 (29%) No

12. Did you follow the plan? (39 responses)
35 (90%) Yes
4   (10%) No

13. Did the plan work? (39 responses)
34 (87%) Yes
5   (13%) No

Comments:
- *After the mold was tested, the plan was developed and followed and it worked successfully.*
- *Disaster was so large, the disaster plan was overlooked by the administration.*
- *The emergency response plan was formulated in 1996. It was not in effect at the time of the explosion, but was in effect for other emergencies. In instances where it did not work as well as planned there was confusion about who was in authority to direct emergency efforts*

Emergency Response Planning Questions 14-26

14. Does your library have an emergency response manual? (67 responses)
50 (75%) Yes
17 (25%) No **(go to question 27)**

15. When was the manual last revised? (46 responses) *(Authors' note: 2005 is the year this survey was administered)*

    9 (19%) 2005
    19 (40%) 2004
    9 (19%) 2003
    3 (6%)   2002
    1 (2%)   2001
    1 (2%)   2000
    3 (6%)   Ten or more years ago
    1 (2%)   Not revised

16. How often is the manual revised? (49 responses)

    30 (61%) As needed
    13 (27%) Annually or 2-3 times/year
    2 (4%)   Every five years
    2 (4%)   Never
    2 (4%)   Other (please specify)
    1 (2%)   Every two years

    Comments:
    - *Library manual focuses on collection recovery, but references and is linked to campus wide emergency response procedures which are also updated annually*
    - *1993 was the last complete revision. Parts have been updated as recently as 2004 (telephone trees and contact information are continually updated).*
    - *The Emergency Response portion was revised in 2004 and the Disaster Plan in 2000.*
    - *Emergency call list is reviewed and revised every six months; the full manual is revised as needed*

17. Who is responsible for the revision? (51 responses)

    16 (31%) Emergency Response Team
    13 (25%) Library Director or Dean
    9 (18%)   Librarian
    6 (16%)   Other
    5 (10%)   Preservation Officer

18. To whom is the manual distributed? (49 responses)

    22 (45%) All library staff and campus safety office
    16 (32%) Other (please list)
    10 (20%) All library staff
    1 (3%)   All library staff, campus safety office and local fire department

    "Other" responses:
    Emergency response team and other campus offices (4)
    All library staff and other campus offices (4)

- *Our Emergency Manual is a short pamphlet distributed to all. The full Disaster Plan is in the hands of the emergency response team and the campus safety officer*
- *All Library staff, campus safety office, campus physical plant office, academic v.p., and one off-campus location (local public library)*
- *Library staff, campus police, Physical Plant, Vice President for Information Resources*

Select library and college staff (3)

- *Each Library unit, each individual on the Telephone Tree (which includes all Library Faculty and department heads, the Chancellor, Provost, Vice Chancellor for Administrative Services and Director of Physical Planning), Library Dean and the University Police Department*

Miscellaneous (6)

- *The Library plan is available in the Director's Office. The campus plan is online and in a couple of places within the library.*
- *Director and Associate Directors, Collection Development Librarian, Preservation Staff, Circulation Desks, Security and Housekeeping, Safety Officer.*
- *The librarians know there is a plan, and it is in the director's file cabinet. They could have a copy of it if they wanted it.*
- *Specific service points, one to each branch, universal distribution as shared electronic document*
- *All university Depts.*

19. Is the manual a comprehensive document for the entire library including branches? (49 responses)

      44 (90%) Yes
       5 (10%) No

20. Are there specific plans for each branch? (41 responses)

      18 (44%) Yes
      23 (56%) No

21. What types of disasters are documented in the manual (mark all that apply)? (51 responses)

      49 (96%) Water, Fire, Weather
      37 (73%) Building structure and systems (HVAC, electrical, plumbing, etc.), Power Failure
      37 (73%) Environmental (mold, earthquake, volcanic eruption, mud slide)
      34 (67%) Bomb threats, Terrorism, Hostage
      34 (67%) Medical, Accident
      26 (51%) Theft, Vandalism, Disruptive or threatening person
      22 (43%) Computer damage or failure, Electronic network disruption

22. Does the manual include an evacuation plan for staff and users? (49 responses)
        38 (78%) Yes
        11 (22%) No

23. Do you rehearse the plan (e.g. conduct fire drills)? How often? (49 responses)
        29 (59%) Yes
        20 (41%) No
           How often?
                Annually or more frequently (19)
                When dictated for the entire campus (3)
                Rarely (2)
                Every two years (1)
                We have fire drills 2 times a year. The emergency phone tree is
                    activated at least once a year.
                Fire drills are held annually, conducted by Campus Security. We have
                    practiced our disaster recovery operation by staging a mock disaster.

24. Does the manual include procedures for dealing with unplanned shut down and recovery of automated systems? (49 responses)
        13 (27%) Yes
        36 (73%) No

25. Does the manual include a list of collection priorities (i.e., what collections or areas of the library should receive attention first, second, etc. in case of an emergency)? (48 responses)
        34 (71%) Yes
        14 (29%) No

26. Does the manual include a list of individuals to contact and/or a staff calling tree? (49 responses)
        49 (100%)   Yes
        0   (0%)   No

Emergency Response Management Questions 27-60

27. Does your library have an Emergency Response Team? (65 responses)
        41 (63%) Yes
        24 (37%) No **(go to question 37)**
        <u>If your library uses a different term for this group please supply the name:</u>
            Disaster Response Team (5)
            Disaster Recovery Team (3)
            Disaster Team (3)
            Emergency Preparedness Team (1)
            Fire Wardens (1)
            Security Team (1)
            Disaster Committee (1)

- *Disaster Response Team - Important distinction; we are not concerned with public safety activities such as bomb threats or disruptive patrons; only with threats to library materials.*
- *The library has an emergency planning committee, not a response team. University has a response team.*
- *Since we are a small staff, the entire staff on duty responds at the time of an emergency.*

28. How many members are on the Emergency Response Team? (42 responses)

    11 (26%) 1-4
    16 (38%) 5-7
    11 (26%) 8-10
     4 (10%) 11 or more

29. What is the composition of the team? (42 responses)

    Selected responses:

        Various library staff (31)

- *Director, department heads.*
- *Library director, librarian, and circulation supervisor*
- *Library staff of all levels divided into functions: Library Director, Services Continuity Team, Communications Manager, Salvage Team.*
- *Director, Assistant Director, Archivist*
- *Librarians and Staff. Special Collections Librarian is the team leader.*
- *Director of Technical Services, Director of Public Services, Asst. Cataloger/End Processor, Public Service Staff member*
- *Documents Librarian (on the second floor), Serials person (located in rear of first floor), Circ Mgr (front of Bldg), Admin. Assist. (front of bldg), Director (Front)*
- *Library Director, Coordinator of Disaster Response, Coordinator of Disaster Recovery Unit, Coordinator for Circulation Unit, Coordinator for Media Services Unit, Coordinator for Reference & Government Documents Unit, Coordinator for Special Collections Unit, Coordinator for Technical Services*
- *Director and Assistant Director, Heads of Cataloging, Preservation, Access Services, paraprofessionals in Preservation and Periodicals*
- *Head of Public Services, Circulation, Media, Music Library staff*
- *University Librarian, Assistant University Librarian, Manager of Access Services, Library Secretary, Technical Services Librarian, Digital Support*
- *Head of Archives & Special Collections (co-chair), Head of Technical Services (co-chair),Head of Public Services, Electronic Resource Librarian, Head of Circulation, Acquisitions Specialist, Administrative Assistant*
- *Dean, Administrative Coordinator, Circulation Coordinators, Librarians, Computer Specialist*

- *Director of library; adjunct reference librarian; and collection development librarian*
- *Assistant Director for Bibliographic Services/ Conservation Officer Team Leader for Reference Services, Head of Access Services*
- *One staff member from each area*
- *Mix of ""exempt"" and ""non-exempt"" library staff, chosen based on their interest, their expertise, and their ability to respond in a timely manner*
- *Designated disaster response leader, library director, serials librarian, library secretary*
- *College Archivist/Preservation Librarian, Archives Assistant, Head of the Schow Science Library, Schow Library Assistant, Head of Circulation, Circulation Assistant, College Librarian, Head of Collection Development, Acquisitions Assistant, Book preparation/Preservation Assistant*
- *University Librarian; Archivist/Special Collections Librarian serve as team leaders; All other staff have been assigned to designated work teams in the areas of salvage, bibliographic control, and supplies.*

Various library staff and other campus administrators or employees (8)
- *Library staff and maintenance workers*
- *3 librarians, library director, director of campus technology*
- *Archivist, Administrative Secretary from dean's office, LTAI from Access Services, LTAI from Bibliographic Services, Instructional Communicator Technical Operator III from Education Technology*
- *Director, Collection Development Librarian, Head of Technical Services, Head of Public Services, Head of Physical Plant, Book conservator, Insurance rep, photographer*
- *3 librarians, security, campus services*
- *Director, Assoc Dir, Recovery Coordinator and two alternates, Chief & Asst. Chief of campus police, 8 subject collection managers (one per floor)*
- *Director of Library, Director of Physical Plant, Safety & Security Liaison, Computing Services Liaison, Communication Coordinator, Volunteer Coordinator, Collections Coordinator*
- *Associate Library Director, Head of Public Services, Assistant to Chief Information Officer, Archivist, Circulation Chief, Technical Services Assistant/Book Repair specialist*

All library staff (2)

Library director only (1)

30. How are the members of the team selected? (41 responses)
    - 19 (46%) Job function and/or Skills and knowledge
    - 8 (20%) Appointed by library director
    - 7 (17%) Volunteers
    - 4 (10%) <u>Other:</u>
        - *Appointed by college administration;*
        - *Head of Preservation in consultation with the Library Director*

- *Two members from each facility who have received training and are willing to take responsibility for responding to disasters, others with needed expertise and/or authority*
- *If you work in the library, you are on the team.*

3 (7%) Head of disaster response team

31. Does the Team have members from outside the library? (41 responses)
    - 10 (24%) Yes
    - 31 (76%) No

32. Does the Team have members from outside the institution? (42 responses)
    - 1 (2%) Yes
    - 41 (98%) No

33. To whom in the library does the team report? (40 responses)
    - 31 (78%) Library director/dean
    - 9 (22%) Other:
        - *Safety Mgr for Campus*
        - *Preservation Librarian/College Archivist*
        - *Library Assistant Director*
        - *CIO Director of Lib*
        - *Preservation officer*
        - *Preservation librarian*
        - *Administrative Coordinator*
        - *Team leaders*
        - *Emergency Preparedness Committee*

34. Does the Team meet regularly? (42 responses)
    - 11 (26%) Yes
    - 31 (74%) No

35. Does the Team have a formal charge? (41 responses)
    - 20 (49%) Yes
    - 21 (51%) No

36. Has the Team received training in emergency response planning and management? (42 responses)
    - 25 (60%) Yes
    - 17 (40%) No

37. Is training offered to (mark all that apply)? (64 responses)
    - 37 (58%) Librarians
    - 36 (56%) Support staff
    - 27 (42%) No training is offered
    - 19 (30%) Student assistants

38.   Indicate the types of training offered (mark all that apply): (39 responses)
        28 (72%) Fire extinguisher use
        23 (59%) Preservation and resource recovery
        12 (31%) Planning
        12 (31%) CPR
         9 (23%) Other

39. How often is training offered? (43 responses)
        14 (33%) Annually or more frequently
        11 (26%) Irregularly, infrequently
         5 (12%) As needed
         2 (5%) Every two years

Other/Comments
- *Whenever consortium offers it.*
- *Fire extinguisher training was conducted once in the past 10 years.*
- *Only once every few years -- we received initial training about 3 years ago which consisted of a short lecture about what we were supposed to do during a fire drill.*
- *We are in the process of developing a training schedule.*
- *Until 2 years ago, CPR and First Aid were offered annually. Recovery of damaged material is offered every few years. Fire extinguisher introduction (not actually putting out a fire) is offered every year or two.*
- *Students receive training at beginning of fall semester. Staff not on a regular basis. Do confer with Physical Plant re: hazardous substances (OSHA) and security office.*
- *Extinguisher training--annually (or biennially)*
- *CPR & First Aid annually, Haz Mat test annually*

40. Who sponsors/schedules the training offered? (39 responses)
         7 (18%) Library staff and/or Director
         6 (15%) Other departments or offices on campus
         5 (13%) Emergency Response Team
         4 (10%) Consortia
         3 (8%) Preservation officer/Curator
         2 (5%) Off-campus organizations such as local fire department
        12 (31%) Various combinations of the above

Comments:
- *University Security does the fire drills. Several librarians do the internal library training. We use videos to support the training.*
- *The library pays for Red Cross training in First aid and CPR for all staff who desire to participate. Typically about half the staff participates.*
- *Library, Director of Environmental Protection & Safety, Director of Campus Safety*

- *Department of Public Safety*
- *Safety/OSHA Compliance person in Operations Dept.*
- *Library, with help from Campus Safety and Security*
- *Coordinator for Staff Development (one of our librarians)*
- *Library director schedules training in conjunction with library consortium disaster response training opportunities.*
- *Library staff utilized security, local fire and police department*
- *Associate Vice President for Facilities*
- *Campus Public Safety and local Fire Department.*
- *1. The library Emergency Disaster Planning Committee. 2. Physical Plant 3. Circulation department staff for student workers*
- *Campus Security and the team leader*
- *Emergency Preparedness Committee, in conjunction with town fire dept.*
- *Campus Police, Solinet*

41. Does your institution have a Risk Assessment office? (65 responses)

    27 (42%) Yes
    38 (58%) No

    Comments:
- *The responsibility rests with the Director of Facilities and Maintenance, the VP for Business Affairs and the Director of Campus Safety.*
- *Yes - Director of Environmental Protection & Safety*
- *We used to have a Risk Assessment Officer but the position was eliminated two years ago.*
- *Safety Services*
- *Internal Control Officer*
- *Essentially Director of Environmental Health & Safety*

42. Does your library have a checklist of people within your institution to contact when an emergency? (65 responses)

    60 (92%) Yes
     5 (8%) No **(go to question 45)**

43. If yes, does it include (mark all that are appropriate)? (60 responses)

    54 (90%) Public Safety
    53 (88%) Physical Plant staff
    26 (43%) Emergency management experts
    24 (40%) Business Office
    14 (23%) Other
    11 (18%) Food Service

44. Is the checklist updated regularly? (62 responses)

    45 (73%) Yes
    17 (27%) No

45. Does the library have a checklist, with locations, of in-building emergency equipment (e.g. wet vacuums, plastic sheeting, etc.)? (64 responses)

         44 (69%) Yes
         20 (31%) No **(go to question 48)**

46. Is the checklist updated regularly? (53 responses)

         36 (68%) Yes
         17 (32%) No

47. Is the checklist in a location accessible to all? (53 responses)

         43 (81%) Yes
         10 (19%) No

48. Does the library have a checklist, with locations, of on-campus emergency equipment (e.g. freezer space, wet vacuums, dehumidifiers, etc.)? (63 responses)

         26 (41%) Yes
         37 (59%) No **(go to question 51)**

49. Is the checklist updated regularly? (48 responses)

         23 (48%) Yes
         25 (52%) No

50. Is the checklist in a location accessible to all? (47 responses)

         22 (47%) Yes
         25 (53%) No

51. Does the library have a checklist, with locations, of off-site emergency recovery suppliers and services? (62 responses)

         38 (61%) Yes
         24 (39%) No **(go to question 54)**

52. Is the checklist of off-site suppliers updated regularly? (49 responses)

         27 (55%) Yes
         22 (45%) No

53. Is the checklist in a location accessible to all? (49 responses)

         29 (59%) Yes
         20 (41%) No

54. Does your library have a checklist of outside consultants who specialize in managing specific types of emergencies? (65 responses)

         37 (58%) Yes
         28 (42%) No

55. Is emergency equipment (e.g., fire extinguishers) within the library regularly inspected? (64 responses)

        61 (95%) Yes
         3 (5%) No

56. Does your library have a written hazard analysis (i.e., protection from predictable losses)? (62 responses)

         8 (13%) Yes
       54 (87%) No

57. Is the location of circuit breakers known to the library staff or the emergency response team? (66 responses)

       50 (76%) Yes
       16 (24%) No

58. Does the library staff or emergency response team have access to the circuit breakers? (65 responses)

       43 (66%) Yes
       22 (34%) No

59. Does your library or institution require that reports be submitted describing emergency events? (65 responses)

       37 (57%) Yes
       28 (43%) No

60. How do you assess your institution's ability to deal with a library disaster? (66 responses)

        5 (8%) Excellent
       34 (51%) Good
       15 (23%) Fair
       12 (18%) Minimal

DOCUMENTS

PLANS: INTRODUCTION, TABLE OF CONTENTS, ORGANIZATION, COMMUNICATION, PRIORITIES

BERTRAND LIBRARY DISASTER PLAN

Disaster Plan #1, June 1994; Revised January 2000; Updated May 2008

Table of Contents

Introduction

A disaster plan is an essential component of sound asset management for university libraries. Many disasters, such as severe weather, cannot be prevented, but sensible planning mitigates damage from such an event if it should occur. On the other hand, rigorous prevention and protection measures *will* prevent many small collection emergencies from escalating into costly big ones.

Most academic institutions recognize that the value of library collections is often second only to the campus buildings. In university libraries, books are estimated at a replacement cost of $75-$100 each. Added to this is the cost of replacing computers and other equipment, software, manuscripts, furnishings, photographs, rare books and other materials. Some of the library's collection may consist of unique, irreplaceable items. Clearly, the most sensible approach is to prevent disasters from striking and to react calmly and logically if the worst should happen.

This disaster plan and set of procedures will guide the staff of the Bertrand Library if it should need to respond to emergencies in the collections. The plan has been developed with the assistance of many staff members and university staff working with experienced consultants. It is, however, a working document and will be revised many times as the Disaster Response Team works with it and makes changes to fit the needs of the library, the staff, and the collections.

The Disaster Response Team is responsible for keeping the plan current and responsive to library collections and concerns. The chair(s) of the team will make any changes necessary and disseminate new information such as staff name changes or new telephone numbers. The team will review the entire plan regularly making suggestions to improve it. All staff will receive revisions and will be educated about how to incorporate them into their own copies of the plan.

The Disaster Response Team is responsible for swift, educated, and calm response to any collection emergency, and will keep itself current about emerging disaster recovery techniques and developments. The team chair(s) will be responsible to the Associate Vice President for Information Services and Resources and will report all changes in the plan as well as any concerns or problems related to disaster preparedness. The chair(s) will communicate frequently and clearly in time of emergency so that the Associate Vice President will be informed about all response and recovery operations.

Emergency Procedures

The Emergency Section of the Disaster Plan contains concise information for any Library staff member who must respond effectively to an emergency in the library. Often staff who have had little or no training in emergency response must initiate the call. They will need directions that are easy to follow and are what the Associate Vice President and the Disaster Response Team have determined are best. The Emergency Section describes precisely how a staff member should respond and who is to be called. Emergency numbers are listed, and a telephone tree is included, as is an alphabetical listing of key people. Laminated copies of these procedures should be disseminated widely and kept where staff can find them easily.

The **Emergency Procedures** are a brief step-by-step set of directions for fire, water, power outage, or vandalism threats to the Library collections.

The **Emergency Priority Notification List** is a listing of the titles, names, and telephone numbers of people in the order in which they are to be notified if there is a collection emergency. Each person has a backup. It is up to these people to keep each other informed about absences or vacations so a gap in communications will not occur in times of emergency. If neither person on the priority notification list can be reached, the caller must proceed to the next person AND notify each successful contact about those who were unreachable. The **Emergency Notification Telephone Tree** is a graphic representation of those who are to be called and how the notification of the emergency will be handled. This assures that communication does not break down. Each person on the tree has a responsibility for ensuring the notification of the next person on the list and must continue calling until someone is reached or the designated backup is contacted. *Communication is key to the success of a disaster response.*

The **Emergency Telephone Numbers** ensure that all staff key to an effective response are listed in alphabetical order so numbers can be located readily at times of stress.

University security experts have been educated about the disaster preparedness process and have contributed to the creation of the plan. Public Safety, Facilities, and the Lewisburg Fire Department have been provided with a copy of the plan.

Emergency Procedures

Post these emergency instructions at all staff telephones and public service points. In case of an emergency that threatens library materials, do these things first.

Appendix C

Disaster Team Member Responsibilities

In this section can be found descriptions of activity categories which will be essential in case of a major emergency. A general description of the responsibilities of the various members of the disaster team follows, and, where appropriate, some examples of tasks which will be involved in the preparation for and response to a library disaster are included.

Every member of the disaster team has the responsibility to select an area in which to develop expertise so to that he/she will be prepared to respond appropriately and effectively to an emergency. At the same time, each member should be acquainted with the plan as a whole so he/she will be able to function as part of the disaster team. In the event of a disaster, each disaster team member will carry out responsibilities which are part of that member's area of expertise and will perform other tasks as assigned by the disaster team leader.

The Disaster Team Leader

The responsibilities of the disaster team leader are over-arching, ensuring that the disaster team members are prepared to respond to an emergency and, then, supervising and coordinating the response and rehabilitation following a disaster. He/she will coordinate and facilitate all activities with the help of those disaster team members whom he/she designates.

In preparation for a disaster
1. Convene and chair meetings of the disaster team.
2. Serve as liaison between the library administration, the university facilities and public safety departments, and the local fire and police departments.
3. Review and update the disaster plan yearly, or more often if necessary, with the help of the team member responsible for documentation.
4. Schedule training sessions for members of the disaster team and for library staff.

In response to a disaster
1. Assess the extent of the disaster and decide if it is necessary to convene the disaster team.
2. Establish a command post.
3. Coordinate decision-making among University Public Safety, the fire department, and library administration.

Documentation

The disaster team member with responsibility for documentation will be prepared to keep records concerning all aspects of the disaster.

In preparation for a disaster
1. Maintain all information relevant to the disaster preparedness and response effort.
2. Develop a system for tracking damage to library materials.

In response to a disaster
1. Take photographs of the disaster site.
2. Note the time and date of all activity involved in the disaster and disaster response effort.
3. Record all decisions made.
4. Collect and compile the damage-assessment notes of the disaster team.
5. Maintain records of library materials removed from the library.

Volunteers

The director of volunteers will be prepared to enlist volunteers if directed by the disaster team leader. He/She will assign volunteers to team members as needed.

In preparation for a disaster
1. Make plans for enlisting volunteers.
2. Maintain a list of potential volunteers.

In response to a disaster
1. Arrange for a rest area for volunteers which will provide restrooms, a snack area, and comfortable seating.
2. Establish a work schedule.
3. Train and supervise volunteers.

Communications

This disaster team member will organize and supervise the communication system for disaster response and recovery.

In the event of a disaster
1. If directed by the team leader, call team members and library staff.
2. Arrange for telephone service for the command post.
3. Act as liaison between disaster team leader and team members.
4. Coordinate all communications during disaster recovery.

Supplies and Services

The disaster team member in charge of supplies and services will maintain the disaster response supplies within the library. He/She will also have information concerning the sources of other necessary equipment and services, should they be required. It is this team member's responsibility to ensure that adequate supplies and equipment are available to those responding to the disaster.

In preparation for a disaster
1. Maintain a list of sources of those supplies which are to be acquired only in case of an emergency.
2. Order and store supplies listed in the disaster plan.
3. Distribute and store plastic drop cloths.
4. Identify and contact potential services, such as commercial freezer facilities.

In Response to a Disaster
1. Distribute supplies from storage area to disaster areas. Acquire new stock as necessary.
2. Provide disaster team leader with information concerning vendors of necessary services.

Monitoring

The team member in charge of monitoring will set up monitoring equipment in the disaster area and the work areas and record the resulting data. This team member will make recommendations for adjusting environmental conditions and will be responsible for recognizing mold growth.

In preparation for a disaster
1. Learn to use monitoring instruments.
2. Learn standards for temperature and humidity.

In the event of a disaster
1. Work with facilities staff to establish desired environmental conditions in disaster area and in work areas.
2. Document temperature and humidity readings in disaster area.
3. Survey affected materials for mold.
4. Survey non-affected materials to establish need for protection. Continue to monitor until building returns to normal.

Washington and Lee University

LEYBURN LIBRARY

Emergency Plan

Lexington Area Conservation Cooperative
A Project Funded by a 1989 Title III LSCA Grant
November 2008

Emergency Salvage of Wet Books and Documents
Emergency Salvage of Moldy Books and Paper
Integrated Pest Management

Introduction

Library staff need to be familiar with the following:
- fire alarm panel
- fire extinguishers
- location of recovery supplies
- emergency numbers list
- telephone tree
- evacuation procedures

A disaster in a library may occur at any time. For this very reason it is
necessary for a library to have a plan which will describe what to do in a
particular emergency, whom to contact, and how to recover from that disaster.
Hard copies of the Emergency Plan are in the Leyburn Library administrative office; at the
Circulation Desk; at the Reference Desk; in the Technical Services area; at
Yolanda Merrill's home; at Physical Plant; at Security; Auxiliary Services; and at the University
Business Office.
This Emergency Plan will be revised and updated once a year by Yolanda Merrill.
After each revision and update, the plan will be circulated to the entire staff
so that everyone can re-familiarize him/herself with its contents and note any
changes.

INTRODUCTION

The purpose of this manual is to provide direction and assistance in the event of an emergency and is to be used by both library staff and students. It provides procedures to follow in the event of fire, bomb threat, disruptive patrons, power failure, weather emergencies, etc. Also included are library evacuation procedures and the responsibilities of each unit or department. The fire marshals from each area are listed in Appendix B. This manual is maintained by the UR Libraries Security Committee and will be reviewed on an annual basis to ensure accurate information and directions.

GENERAL SECURITY GUIDELINES

1. IF YOU OPEN A DOOR, CLOSE IT! Tug doors closed. Doors can easily appear closed but not be securely latched.
2. IF YOU UNLOCK A DOOR, LOCK IT!
3. Report any problems with doors or locks to the Library Administrative Assistant for notification to University Facilities.
4. A Security Checklist of external and internal doors will be maintained by the Night Supervisor; and is attached as Appendix D. This list helps to track the doors that are wired to the alarm system and those that are not.
5. Keep work areas well-defined and restricted to staff. Do not allow patrons to remain in unauthorized areas.

6. Keep the Campus Police number at each phone.
7. When the Library is closed to the public, absolutely no one but regularly employed, permanent Library faculty and staff should be allowed in the building for any reason without specific authorization from the University Librarian.

Library Keys

Library keys should not be loaned to anyone except under very unusual circumstances. Every effort should be made to avoid situations in which students need to be given Library keys. Keep all Library keys not in your personal possession secured at all times.

No one but Circulation staff members should hand out or receive Circulation keys to Library areas. (Student assistants from other departments should not go into the key/money drawer at Circulation. Circulation is responsible for these monies and the accounts are closed and balanced each morning. Control over access to this drawer must be maintained.)

In the event that the Circulation submaster must be borrowed, it must be returned to Circulation immediately after the door in question is opened.

All access points to the roof must remain locked at all times, not only for reasons of safety but to limit the University's liability.
   a) Digital Production Services closet door

b) Periodicals stairwell roof hatch closet door (located in interior stair well between Upper Commons and Bound Periodicals)

c) Top tower room door

ALARMS

Fire

The alarm board is located on the wall in the Circulation work area. According to Campus Police, Library staff should not silence fire alarms due to Fire Department regulations. Red lights normally are illuminated for all the zones indicated on the old board. When a fire alarm occurs, the panel will "beep" and indicate the trouble area. Alarm horns will also sound inside the Library. When the alarm horn sounds, library staff should begin evacuation procedures immediately.

Door Alarms

The door alarm panel is located on the outside wall adjacent to the staff passageway leading to the Main Service Desk. Under normal conditions a red light indicates that the system is armed. In the event that someone exits through an alarmed door, local alarms will sound at the door and at the panel. The alarm location will be indicated on the display board of the panel.

When a door alarm sounds, it may be silenced by following the alarm instructions posted near the alarm panel. Check the door in question, close it firmly, then return to the panel to clear it. Clear the alarm by using the keypad and then rearm the system using the posted instructions Please note that the BML sub-master key is needed to silence the local alarms at doors 2 and 7. Also, the police need to be called to silence alarm door 5.

STAFFING IN THE LIBRARIES DURING WEATHER OR OTHER EMERGENCIES

The libraries' response to weather or other emergencies when the University is declared closed will vary depending upon the circumstances. Each is explained below:

If the University closes on a weekday during the fall or spring semester and ALL classes are canceled

- The University is closed if and only if University authorities announce the closing through the news media, voicemail broadcast messages, etc.
- If possible, when students are on campus, the Library and Information Services should provide basic services even if the University is closed. That means that managers should work out a plan to have coverage for those areas that provide customer or patron services. Boatwright Memorial Library should be open if at all possible. If students are on campus this will give them a place to work and study. The IS Help Desk and the Jepson labs should be open. Opening the library, the Help Desk and the labs can be accomplished with a minimum number of staff augmented by student workers. Non-exempt staff should not report unless explicitly asked to report.

- XXX should be prepared with copies of student managers' work schedules and phone numbers so that they can arrange student staffing of circulation and the MRC.
- Boatwright Library will open at 8:00 AM (or as soon as possible thereafter) if staffing can be arranged.
- Boatwright Library will remain open for its normally scheduled hours provided that staffing can be arranged for all hours.
    - If reference or MRC hours must be abbreviated because of lack of student workers, those students working should prepare and post signs conveying that information.
    - If it appears that it will not be possible to sustain hours continuously until the normally scheduled closing time XXX will confer by telephone with XXX.
    - XXX will arrange on-call remote reference service for at least part of the day. She will call xxx-xxxx and explain to the student manager procedures for anyone who wishes to use this service. The student manager will share that information with other student workers on duty at that time and leave this information in writing for others who will work later in the day.
- If XXX can arrange student staffing for the Music Library, she should do so from 10:00 AM until the normal scheduled closing time. If student staffing cannot be arranged until the scheduled closing time, then the Music Library should close early and student workers should post signs conveying that information.
- No staff member will be required to use vacation time for time not present at work on a day when the University is declared closed.

If the University closes on a weekday during the fall break, the spring break, winter break, or during the summer (NOTE: winter break begins at the conclusion of fall semester final exams and concludes at the start of classes for the spring semester.)

- The University is closed if and only if University authorities announce the closing through the news media, voicemail broadcast messages, etc.
- The libraries will be closed.
- Nobody should report to work.
- No staff member will be required to use vacation time for time not present at work on a day when the University is declared closed.

If the University cancels classes for part but not all of a weekday during the fall or spring semester (NOTE: This is most likely to occur when weather conditions turn bad during the course of the day and evening classes are canceled.)

- If staff are free to leave work early without using vacation time for the remainder of their work schedule, the University authorities will announce this, most likely through a voicemail broadcast message.

- If the University does not make such an announcement and a staff member concludes that weather conditions are such that he/she should leave work early rather than risk hazardous travel conditions, that individual must use vacation time for the time not worked.

On Weekends

- If weather conditions are such that staff scheduled to work in Boatwright circulation on a Saturday or Sunday judge that traveling to campus would involve risk they deem unacceptable, they should call XXX and work with him to arrange staffing.
- If weather conditions are such that staff scheduled to work in Boatwright reference on a Saturday or Sunday judge that traveling to campus would involve risk they deem unacceptable, they should inform XXX and decide what information needs to be communicated to circulation staff.

In the Evenings

- If weather conditions deteriorate and a staff member concludes that those conditions are such that he/she should leave work early rather than risk hazardous travel conditions, that individual should:
  - o Circulation staff should arrange student staffing for scheduled hours.

  Reference staff should inform circulation staff and identify options (if there are any) for obtaining reference service.

Introduction

A.   Purpose

This Crisis Management Protocols (CMP) Plan is designed for use by the (Library) to respond to an actual crisis event. Ongoing and overall University emergency response operations and University recovery operations are defined in the University's Crisis Management Plan (CMP) and Business Continuity Plan (BCP).

All of these plans have important specific purposes and are intended for use in concurrence to lessen the extent of injuries and limit equipment, material, and property damage.

B.   Mission

The University and the (Library) will respond to an emergency situation in a safe, effective and timely manner. University personnel and equipment will be utilized to accomplish the following priorities:

Priority I: Protection of human life

Priority II: Support of health, safety, and security services

Priority III: Protection of University assets

Priority IV: Maintenance of University services

Priority V: Assessment of damages

Priority VI: Restoration of general campus operations

C.   University Incident Commander

The Crisis Management Protocols Plan for the University operates under the "Incident Command System" – a system utilized by FEMA (Federal Emergency Management Agency) and many other organizations. Under this system, a single Incident Commander (IC) directs all University resources. The IC is not necessarily a Crisis Management Team member. The IC will report to the University president and coordinate with the Crisis Management Team (CMT). Although the University Incident Commander (IC) may consult with other individuals, it is imperative that all employees follow the decisions made by the University Incident Commander (IC).

The University Incident Commander (IC) is the most qualified available individual for the particular incident/situation (i.e., personnel from the Department of Campus Security, personnel from the Physical Plant, personnel from the Environmental Safety office, personnel from the Information Technology Services department, personnel from Counseling and Health Services, etc.).

Revision: January 2009

D.   Communications

Plan Activation

In case of any type of campus emergency, individuals making the discovery should **first move to a safe location and then contact the Department of Campus Security**. The Department of Campus Security officer on duty should follow standard department operating procedures, establish the Incident Command System (ICS), become the initial Incident Commander (IC) and contact civil authorities (San Antonio Police Department, San Antonio Fire Department, etc.), as warranted for the situation.

If the emergency warrants, the Department of Campus Security officer should communicate immediately with the Incident Commander (IC). **The Incident Commander (IC) will assess the situation and direct the Department of Campus Security dispatcher to activate the Crisis Management Team (CMT) call tree and summon the necessary University personnel required to contain and control the emergency.** During a crisis situation members of the Crisis Management Team (CMT) should be prepared to report to the Emergency Operations Center (EOC) or other location as directed by the Incident Commander (IC) (See Attachment C).

Media Communications

Communication procedures and authorities are detailed in the Business Continuity Plan (BCP) and in the University Communications office Crisis Management Plan. **The individuals designated in these plans are the only individuals officially authorized to represent the University to the news media.**

Communications with Parents and Relatives

Communication procedures and authorities are detailed in the Business Continuity Plan (BCP) and in the Executive Staff Crisis Management Plan. **The individuals designated in these plans are the only individuals authorized to communicate with parents and relatives of students.**

Communications with Faculty, Staff and their Families

Communication procedures and authorities are detailed in the Business Continuity Plan (BCP) and in the Executive Staff Crisis Management Plan. **The individuals designated in these plans are the only individuals authorized to communicate with faculty, staff, and their family members.**

Information

For emergency information regarding events that are affecting or may impact normal University operations, contact the Emergency Hotline 888-xxxx (888-xxxxxxx) or visit the University Web site www.trinity.edu/emergencyprep.

The Department of Campus Security and/or members of the Crisis Management Team (CMT) will convey emergency information to the campus community utilizing a number of various communications systems available (i.e., VoIP telephones, TrinAlert system, campus e-mail, public address systems, runners, etc.), as appropriate to the specific emergency.

Revision: January 2009

Trinity University

TABLE OF CONTENTS

Natural Disasters:

Man-Made Disasters:

Attachments:

EMERGENCY NUMBERS

ALL EMERGENCIES Campus Security Ext.5900

Ambulance 944-1111 or 9-911

Campus Operations Ext. 5904

Drug Help line 1-800-DRUGHELP (1-800-378-4435)

Fire Dept. Jackson Fire Dept. 601-969-3333

Hospital Baptist Medical Center 601-968-1000

Inclement Weather Info. Ext. 8998

Methodist Health Care 601-376-1000

Police Jackson Police Dept. 601-960-1234

St. Dominic Health Sys. 601-982-0121

Security Campus Security Ext. 5900

Jim Glenn, Director of Security Ext. 5929

EMERGENCY TELEPHONE LIST

When an emergency occurs and after the necessary authorities (Security - Ext.5900, Fire Dept. 969-3333, Campus Operations Ext.5904) have been contacted, the person on duty at the Circulation Desk should contact the next person-in-charge. Call the person at the top of the list. If unavailable, call the next person on the list and so forth until someone is reached.

Gretchen Cook: ### (cell) or ### (home)
Margaret Root: ### (home) or ### (cell)
Chris Cullnane: ### (home)
David Browne: ### (cell)
Melissa Dennis: ### (home)
Vicki Miner: ### (home) or ### (cell)
Brinda Stocker: ### (home)

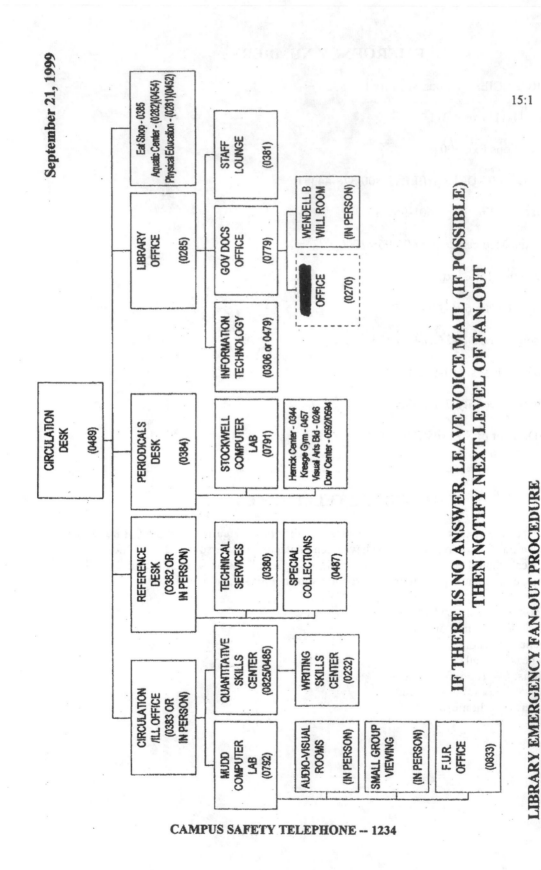

CIRCULATION DESK (0489)

EAT SHOP - 0385
Aquatic Center - (0282)(0454)
Physical Education - (0281)(0452)

LIBRARY OFFICE (0285)

STAFF LOUNGE (0381)

GOV DOCS OFFICE (0779)

WENDELL B WILL ROOM (IN PERSON)

OFFICE (0270)

INFORMATION TECHNOLOGY (0306 or 0479)

PERIODICALS DESK (0384)

STOCKWELL COMPUTER LAB (0791)

Herrick Center - 0344
Kresge Gym - 0457
Visual Arts Bld - 0246
Dow Center - 0592/0594

REFERENCE DESK (0382 OR IN PERSON)

TECHNICAL SERVICES (0380)

SPECIAL COLLECTIONS (0487)

CIRCULATION /ILL OFFICE (0383 OR IN PERSON)

QUANTITATIVE SKILLS CENTER (0825/0485)

WRITING SKILLS CENTER (0232)

MUDD COMPUTER LAB (0792)

AUDIO-VISUAL ROOMS (IN PERSON)

SMALL GROUP VIEWING (IN PERSON)

F.U.R. OFFICE (0833)

**IF THERE IS NO ANSWER, LEAVE VOICE MAIL (IF POSSIBLE)
THEN NOTIFY NEXT LEVEL OF FAN-OUT**

LIBRARY EMERGENCY FAN-OUT PROCEDURE
WEEKDAYS

CAMPUS SAFETY TELEPHONE -- 1234

**MEMBERS OF THE DISASTER RECOVERY TEAM FOR CLEMENS LIBRARY
AND ASSIGNED RESPONSIBILITIES**

TEAM ADMINISTRATOR/DIRECTOR OF RECOVERY COMMITTEE –**Director of
Libraries, Media and Archives**
Makes decisions that require financial authority such as what to salvage and at what cost;
what information is needed to file insurance claims; where to concentrate efforts of other team
members.

COLLECTION MANAGEMENT - **OSB/Collection Development Librarian, Associate
Director for Media Services and Associate Director for Technical Services**
Makes decisions about merits of replacement versus restoration for particular items.

TEAM RECORDER/RECORD KEEPER/CATALOGER- **Associate Director for Technical
Services**
Responsible for all records generated during the recovery operation such as insurance records,
alphanumeric stack records, storage records, photographic records of damage. Identifies and
notes disposition of all materials handled in the salvage operation.

COMMUNICATIONS MANAGER –**Associate Director for Public Services**
This individual would command a control center to provide communications for the entire
recovery operation. Duties might include handling incoming and outgoing messages and
communicating with outside resources as defined in the disaster plan. Coordinates internal and
external information needs and handles public relations (media).

BUILDING MANAGER/PHYSICAL PLANT/MAINTENANCE –**Facility Manager**
This individual would supply specific information concerning the building such as blueprints,
utility locations, alternate power sources. Coordinates service people as found in the disaster
plan: electricians, plumbers, carpenters, renovators and professional cleaners, pest control
experts and technical people like chemists.

ADDITIONAL MEMBERS:
INSURANCE REPRESENTATIVE - assists with damage claims - **Mahowald Insurance.**

PHOTOGRAPHER - records disaster and recovery process. A photographer attached to
the institution should document the initial disaster scene and the subsequent recovery. It is
less satisfactory to retrieve pictures from any media coverage of the event because a media
photographer covers the scene as news. Contact: **Communication & Marketing Services**

BOOK CONSERVATOR - This individual should be knowledgeable about the recovery
procedures for fire and water-damaged materials. Duties might include evaluating the extent
of damage; helping train volunteers and staff on proper handling of damaged materials;
coordinating all recovery operations. **Staff Preservationist**

FIRST RESPONSE TEAM

A true library disaster would result in damage to the building and collections. In this event, the First Response Team would be the first to re-enter the building. The Team would assess damage and determine immediate and long-term needs and plans, referring to the Disaster Response Plan for guidance. The library phone tree would be used to communicate with the rest of the Belk Library staff and to notify them of recovery plans.

The First Response Team should include the following Belk Library staff:
1) Library Director
2) Director of Campus Technology
3) Coordinator of Public Services
4) Coordinator of Technical Services and Archives
5) Coordinator of Serials and Documents
6) Library Disaster Coordinator

In 2003-2004, these staff members and contact numbers are:

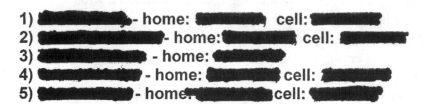

Disaster Plan notebooks are in the homes and offices of the First Response Team. Notebooks are also available in the campus offices of Ken Mullen, Assistant Vice President for Business and Finance, and Allen Poe, Campus Safety and Security Officer, and at the library Information Desk.

DISASTER RESPONSE PLAN

Issues:

o First Response Team
o First Response Plan

First Response Plan:

The priorities for the First Response Team will be:

1) <u>Safety</u>. Necessary assistance will be provided for emergency crews if there are injuries. With the assistance of Campus Security and the Physical Plant, the safety of the library building will be determined.

2) <u>Assessment of needs</u>. The team will check all areas of the building and collections to determine immediate needs.

3) <u>Developing a plan of action</u>. Using standard disaster response guidelines, the team will develop a reasonable plan of action for beginning a disaster response. These guidelines are outlined on the following pages.

4) <u>Communication</u>. The team will use the established library phone tree to keep the rest of the library staff informed.

5) <u>Protection of the library collection</u>. In the event of major water damage, the immediate response should be to lower the temperature and humidity in the building to prevent mold. Running the air conditioning system, by generator if necessary, is important. Running dehumidifiers is also helpful. This will allow time to begin a recovery effort.

6) <u>Documentation of damage</u>. For insurance claims purposes, photographs must be taken of all damage to the building and to library collections.

III. SALVAGE PRIORITIES

In the event of a disaster that involves the whole building or portions of it, collection materials should be protected, transferred to a safe location, or salvaged in the priority order listed below. The priority levels are:

Priority 1 = Highest
Priority 2 = Important, Save after Highest
Priority 3 = Average, Save after Highest and Important
Priority 4 = Not Priority, save if you can
Priority 5 = Lowest Priority

As a result of a survey of the Subject Specialists for each floor the following priorities were identified:

<u>Information Resources</u> - ██████, Systems Administrator ██████
    Priority 1 - All office processors, library servers and hard drives.

<u>Audio-Visual Center</u> – ██████ Instructional Media Specialist ██████
    Priority 1 – Hardware (laptop computers, visual presenter, digital pallette, multimedia projectors)
    Priority 2 – Software (VHS, DVD, computer)
    Priority 3 – A/V equipment (TV, VCR, sound equipment, audio recorders)
    Priority 4 - Albums, filmstrips, 16mm films, slides

<u>Floor 2</u> - ██████, Subject Specialist ██████
    Priority 1 - Bound Periodicals and Microforms
    Priority 2 - Reference
    Priority 3 - Circulating Materials
    Priority 4 - Indexes and Current Periodicals

<u>Floor 3</u> - ██████, Subject Specialist ██████
    Priority 1 - Bound Periodicals, Reference (particularly on Alabama History); Circulating books on Alabama (Call number F320 through F330) and Atlases.
    Priority 2 - Special Collection materials (Library of American Civilization; American Culture Series; British State Papers and Draper Manuscripts).
    Priority 3 - Current Periodicals
    Priority 4 – Circulating Materials
    Priority 5 - Indexes

<u>Floor 4</u> - ██████, Subject Specialist ██████
    Priority 1 - Reference
    Priority 2 - Bound Periodicals and ABI/Inform CD-Rom collection

III-1

Priority 3 - Current Periodicals
Priority 4 - Microforms, Indexes and Circulating Materials

Floor 5 – ▒▒▒▒▒▒▒▒, Subject Specialist (▒▒▒▒▒▒▒)
    Priority 1 - Reference
    Priority 2 - Current Periodicals, Bound Periodicals, Circulating Materials, in particular the Education Materials (Call number "L") and Juvenile Collection (Call Number "J", "JUV")
    Priority 3 - Circulating Materials, in particular the Physical Education materials (Call Number "GV") and Textbook materials (Call Numbers "TC" and "TEXT")
    Priority 4 - Microforms including the ERIC collection
    Priority 5 - Textbooks for adoption

Floor 6 - ▒▒▒▒▒▒▒▒, Subject Specialist (▒▒▒▒▒▒▒)
    Priority 1 - Reference
    Priority 2 - Bound Periodicals
    Priority 3 - Current Periodicals
    Priority 4 - Microforms, Indexes and Circulating Materials

Floor 7 - ▒▒▒▒▒▒▒, Subject Specialist (▒▒▒▒▒▒▒)
    Priority 1 - Reference and Circulating Materials
    Priority 2 - Bound Periodicals
    Priority 3 - Current Periodicals
    Priority 4 - Indexes
    Priority 5 - Microforms

Floor 9 - ▒▒▒▒▒▒▒▒, Subject Specialist (▒▒▒▒▒▒▒)
    Priority 1 - Reference
    Priority 2 - Bound Periodicals
    Priority 3 - Current Periodicals
    Priority 4 - Microforms, Circulating Materials and large books located across from the librarian's office.
    Priority 5 - Indexes

Floor 10 - ▒▒▒▒▒▒▒▒, Subject Specialist (▒▒▒▒▒▒▒)
    Priority 1 - Alabama Gallery and Reference
    Priority 2 - Bound Periodicals
    Priority 3 - Indexes and Current Periodicals
    Priority 4 - Microforms and Circulating Materials

Collection Priorities in Dealing with Damaged Materials

In most instances, damaged circulating materials--print, microform, and audiovisual--will be replaced rather than restored. Replacement will cost considerably less in time and money than restoration. Stabilization of the library's temperature and humidity will require quick removal of wet materials from the building. Documenting which materials have been damaged will be important for insurance purposes.

How the library's staff documents these damaged materials will depend on the nature and extent of the damage. Using the library's computer system, the staff can produce a shelf list for the range of damaged materials to note their status in our on-line catalog and to create a bibliography. The bibliography will help with the replacement and deselection of the materials.

Materials that are irreplaceable or that possess high scholarly, historical, aesthetic, or monetary value will need to be examined soon after re-entering the building. Steps to salvage these items will need to be taken quickly.

The orientation for each collection during disaster recovery shall be as follows:

General book collection—replacement

Reference collection—replacement

Microfilm collection—replacement

Audiovisual collection—replacement

Archives—*restoration*

Rare Books Room—*restoration*, probably with greater selectivity than with Archives

DOCUMENTS

RESPONSES TO EMERGENCIES

Disaster Response Steps

Disaster response covers the initial phase of the Library's reaction to a collection emergency. Depending upon the extent of the disaster, the time represented may be a few hours or several days. In the catastrophic Los Angeles Central Public Library fire in 1987, the response phase lasted for two weeks. This phase is not over until the damaged collections have been removed and stabilized and the rest of the collections are protected from further damage. Then, planning can proceed and decisions can be made for how recovery will be undertaken.

The disaster response section contains the information needed by the Disaster Team for a fast and effective response to a collection emergency. The section has been planned carefully to assist the Disaster Team members with their responsibilities. It is often difficult to think clearly after disaster has struck collections. The Team and the consultants have asked many questions to ensure smooth communication and sound decisions related to the emergency and the collections affected. The section covers who will assess the damage to the collections, how response is initiated, as well as the activation of plans for services, supplies and experts. Names of backup team members are supplied. Although training in response steps is best for any Team, the directions supplied in this section should make it possible for any staff member to understand what must be done.

Immediately following this page is a brief guide for disaster response which may be used as a check list during a collection emergency.

A Brief Guide for Immediate Disaster Response

1. Who is in charge?

2. What is the extent of the disaster?
- What materials are affected?
- How many materials are affected?
- Which high priority materials are affected?

3. How serious is the damage to materials?

4. Is the cause of the disaster being addressed?

5. Are the collections not affected being protected from potential damage?

6. Have all necessary library staff been notified?

7. Have all necessary facilities, security, and insurance staff been notified?

8. What supplies, equipment, services, and/or space will be needed?
- Are required supplies available or will additional supplies or services have to be ordered or contacted? Who is doing this?
- Will extra space be required to work or air dry or store materials? Who is arranging for this?
- Will additional staff or volunteers be required and trained? Who is doing this?

- Will transportation be needed to move collections? Who is taking care of this?

9. How are affected materials going to be dealt with?
- Are freezers needed for stabilization?
- What recovery methods are appropriate?

10. How will service be restored and when? Who is charge of this?

Disaster Response Steps

1. **Control source of disaster and eliminate hazards**
2. **Assess the disaster situation**
3. **Set up a command post**

Library: Shipping and Receiving

Backup:

CCS Conference Room

4. **Convene disaster team members**

Library: Shipping and Receiving

Backup:

CCS Conference Room

5. **Assess and document initial damage to collections on site**
6. **Protect undamaged collections and provide security**
7. **Remove water and control the environment**
8. **Set priorities for salvage (See Collection Priority List)**
9. **Decided upon stabilization and recovery needs**
10. **Activate plans for supplies**
11. **Activate plans for volunteers**
12. **Activate plans for space**
13. **Activate plans for services**
14. **Document all activity**
15. **Set up communications**
16. **Call in consultants if necessary**

WHAT TO DO IN AN EMERGENCY

FIRE
If you discover a fire, activate the nearest fire alarm and **Telephone ext. 6000.**
If the alarm is activated **Telephone ext. 5050.**
Evacuate the library.
Do not use elevators.

BOMB THREAT
Telephone ext. 6000.
Evacuate the library, if so instructed by Police.

INOPERATIVE ELEVATORS
Daytime: Telephone ext. 5255.
Nights and weekends: Telephone 5050 (University Police).
Do **NOT** attempt to remove people from the elevator. Tell them they are safe and help is on the way.

DISRUPTIVE/ INAPPROPRIATE BEHAVIOR
Telephone 5050
If reported by a patron, ask him/her to stay and talk with Police. If he/she will not stay, get their contact information and complete description of the incident.
Complete the Library's incident report form.

OBSCENE PHONE CALLS
Hang up the phone.
If the caller is persistent, contact University Police at ext. 5050.

EMA SIRENS
If unsure as to reason for siren, call **University Police at 5050.**

THEFT AND VANDALISM
Telephone 5050
If reported by patron, ask him/her to stay and talk with police. If patron will not stay, get contact information and complete description of incident.
Complete the Library's incident report form

WEATHER WARNING
In the event of a weather warning, the University Police will call and advise that staff and patrons take shelter.
Make an announcement that a WARNING has been issued and that everyone should take shelter in the basement.

MEDICAL EMERGENCY
Telephone ext. 6000.
Describe the emergency and request medical assistance.
Complete the Library's incident report form.

POWER OUTAGE
Telephone ext. 5050.
Patrons should remain on the floors.
The staff should rely on emergency lighting and flashlights as needed.

COMPUTER /SYSTEM PROBLEMS
Telephone ext. 8180 (Library Systems Administrator)
If the Systems Administrator does not answer, contact the Circulation Desk. Circulation staff will contact library administrators and/or University Police.

RESPONSE PROCEDURES: MOLD

Spores of mold and mildew are found almost everywhere. All they require are the proper conditions--moisture, temperature, nutrients, and often darkness or dim light--to proliferate. Media such as paper, cloth, leather, and adhesives may be consumed or stained by many types of mold. The combination of temperature and humidity is the most critical factor. General cleanliness and the removal of dust and dirt reduce the risk of infestation, and good air circulation is helpful in avoiding a mold outbreak.

When the temperature reaches 70 degrees Fahrenheit and relative humidity is near 70%, conditions are optimal for growth and reproduction of most types of mold. Any rise in these levels creates an environment conducive to mold and mildew growth, and they may "blossom" within 48 to 72 hours. The absence of visible growth at low temperatures does not indicate the death of spores, but merely that they have gone dormant.

A mold outbreak may occur during routine times if temperature and humidity controls are not adequate, but the risk is greater after a flood or other water damage. In the event of a mold outbreak, take the following actions:

1. If mold is on a few isolated items:

   a. Place items in freezer bags, located in the lobby.

   b. Call the Recovery Coordinater, ███████████, x5762 (office) or ████████ (home).

   c. If the Recovery Coordinator is not available, leave a message and put the items (enclosed in plastic freezer bags) in a freezer.

2. If mold is discovered in whole stack ranges, drawers, or rooms, call:

████████████ University Librarian	Office: 5248	Home: ████████
████████████ Head of Library Services	Office: 5757	Home: ██████
████████████ Recovery Coordinator	Office: 5762	Home: ██████
████████████ Disaster Team	Office: 5251	Home: ████████
████████████ Disaster Team	Office: 5244	Home: ██████

IV-12

Office: ████   Home: ████

Disaster Team

Librarian whose floor is affected.

3. Obtain appropriate supplies from the disaster supply kit, located in the lobby. Wear appropriate protective gear such as gloves and respirators.

4. Seal materials in garbage bags, located in the lobby.

5. When dealing with a moderate- or large-scale mold problem, keep air movement to a minimum, since air currents spread mold spores to other, unaffected collections.

   • Do not use fans in the area.
   • Minimize the opening and closing of doors.
   • If feasible, block off return air vents so spores are not spread into the air-handling system and to other storage areas.

6. Transfer all infected materials to an isolation room in such a manner that other areas will not be affected because of the transportation of materials.

7. Immediately and thoroughly sterilize the affected storage area(s), including the climate control system where possible.

8. Determine whether the affected items must be retained. If not, consider discarding, photocopying, or microfilming.

9. If the items must be salvaged, consult a conservator or preservation specialist when dealing with severely affected materials. If the number of affected items is small, they may be treated in-house. See instructions in Lois Price's *Managing a Mold Invasion: Guidelines for Disaster Response* for detailed instructions. (Appendix C5, Mold Information.)

10. Check materials periodically (at least monthly) for evidence of new or recurrent growth. Carry out these inspections for one year following the infestation.

RESPONSE PROCEDURES: BOMB THREAT

1. **Keep the caller on the telephone, if possible, and gather information noted on the Bomb Report Form (immediately following these instructions).**
    Copies of this form will be kept at the Circulation Desk.

2. **Immediately call University Police (ext. 6000).**

3. **Evacuate building if so instructed by the University Police.**

    a. The following announcement should be made over the P.A. system:
        "An emergency situation exists. Please exit the building immediately."

    b. In the event of an emergency evacuation, library staff members should not return to their work area but should immediately begin evacuating people in the area in which they are located.

    c. Each floor librarian is responsible for making sure that everyone on the floor has been evacuated, including occupants of carrels, rest rooms, or other enclosed areas. When two or more librarians share a floor, evacuation responsibility will be divided according to a pre-approved plan for that floor. If a floor is without supervision, it will be the responsibility of the librarian assigned to the floor above, University Librarian, Head of Library Services, or senior staff member to make sure the unattended floor is evacuated. Before leaving, the senior person on the floor should ensure that all persons on the floor are gone.

4. **Library staff should meet in the designated staging area (Church Street (East) entrance steps) and report to the University Librarian, Head of Library Services, or Senior Staff Member when they have cleared the building.**
    The University Librarian, Head of Library Services, or Senior Staff Member will be on the entrance steps and will have a check-off sheet for all areas. The *Emergency Evacuation Check List* will be kept on a clipboard at the Circulation Desk. Staff should check in with the person with the clipboard. They should report as to the status of their areas and any pertinent information about unchecked areas, individuals in the building, or other problems.

5. **Upon exiting the building, staff should go to the staging area (Church Street (East) entrance steps) and remain far enough away from the building to allow emergency personnel unimpeded access to the building.**
    AT NO TIMES SHOULD LIBRARY STAFF REENTER THE BUILDING WHILE AN EMERGENCY EXISTS. STAFF MAY REENTER THE BUILDING WHEN AUTHORIZED TO DO SO BY THE APPROPRIATE INDIVIDUAL. For the Houston Cole Library, this individual will be the University Librarian, Head of Library Services, or Senior Staff Member. DO NOT REENTER THE BUILDING UNLESS THIS INDIVIDUAL HAS INDICATED PERMISSION TO DO SO.

6. **When the building has been cleared for reentry, all emergency exits must be checked to make sure that they are closed and operational.**

BOMB THREAT REPORT FORM

Date: _____ Time: _____
Person Receiving the Call: _____
Exact Words of Caller:

_____
_____
_____
_____
_____
_____
_____
_____

Ask the caller the following questions:

    a. Who placed the bomb? _____
    b. What does it look like?

        ☐ Round   ☐ Square   ☐ Package   ☐ Briefcase   ☐ Other _____

    c. What kind of bomb is it? _____
    d. What will cause it to explode? _____
    e. What is your name? _____
    f. When is it going to explode? _____
    g. Exactly where is the bomb? _____
    h. Why was it placed? _____

Other information to aid in the investigation and search:

    a. Voice characteristics of the caller

        ☐ Male ☐ Female ☐ Young ☐ Middle Age ☐ Old ☐ Excited ☐ Deep

        ☐ High Pitch ☐ Soft ☐ Raspy ☐ Loud ☐ Intoxicated ☐ Calm ☐ Angry

        ☐ Crying ☐ Normal ☐ Familiar ☐ Laughing ☐ Cracking ☐ Ragged

        ☐ Disguised ☐ Deep Breathing ☐ Other _____

    b. Speech

        ☐ Fast ☐ Stutter ☐ Distorted ☐ Well Spoken ☐ Slow ☐ Lisp ☐ Nasal

        ☐ Distinct ☐ Taped Message ☐ Foul ☐ Slurred ☐ Irrational ☐ Incoherent

        ☐ Other _____

    c. Background noise

        ☐ Street (Cars, Buses, Etc.) ☐ House (Dishes, TV, Etc.) ☐ Motor (Fan, A/C, Etc.)

        ☐ Factory Machinery ☐ Long Distance ☐ Animal Noises ☐ Phone Booth ☐ Clear

        ☐ PA System ☐ Local Call ☐ Airplanes ☐ Voices ☐ Music ☐ Static

        ☐ Other _____

    d. Other Information: _____

IV-7

CALHOUN COUNTY EMERGENCY MANAGEMENT AGENCY

Evacuation Routes and Reception/Mass Care Locations

P = Primary Route   **A = Alternate Route**

ZONE

A-1   P: Quickest route to I-20 towards Atlanta. (Host: Lee County)
A: Quickest route to AL Hwy 9 towards Centre. (Host: Madison County)

A-1A P: Quickest route to I-20 towards Birmingham. (Host: Jefferson County)
A: Quickest route to AL Hwy 9 towards Centre. (Host: Madison County)

A-2   P: Quickest route to US 432 towards Gadsden. (Host: Jefferson County)
A: Quickest route to AL Hwy 9 towards Centre. (Host: Madison County)

A-3   P: Quickest route to I-20 towards Atlanta. (Host: Lee County)
A: Quickest route to AL Hwy 9 towards Centre. (Host: Madison County)

A-4   P: Quickest route to AL Hwy 9 towards Centre. (Host: Madison County)
A: Quickest route to I-20 towards Atlanta. (Host: Lee County)

A-5   P: Quickest route to US 431 towards Gadsden. (Host: Jefferson County)
A: Quickest route to AL Hwy 9 towards Centre. (Host: Madison County)

A-6 P: Quickest route to AL Hwy 9 towards Centre. (Host: Madison County)
A: Quickest route to AL Hwy 9 towards Heflin. (Host: Lee County)**

A-7   P: Quickest route to AL Hwy 9 towards Centre. (Host: Madison County)
A: Quickest route to US 431 towards Gadsden. (Host: Jefferson County)

A-8   P: Quickest route to AL Hwy 9 towards Centre. (Host: Madison County)
A: Quickest route to Hwy 278 towards Gadsden. (Host: Jefferson County)

A-9   P: Quickest route to AL Hwy 9 towards Centre. (Host: Madison County)
A: Quickest route to Hwy 278 towards Gadsden. (Host: Jefferson County)

A-10 P: Quickest route to AL Hwy 9 towards Centre. (Host: Madison County)
A: Quickest route to AL Hwy 9 towards Heflin. (Host: Lee County)

B-1   P: Quickest route to I-20 towards Birmingham. (Host: Jefferson County)
A: Quickest route to I-20 towards Atlanta. (Host: Lee County)

** Houston Cole Library is in Zone A-6.

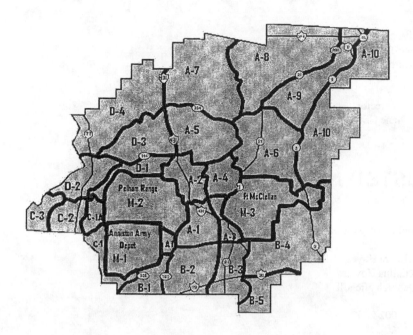

CALHOUN COUNTY ZONAL MAP

If you need help determining your zone,

call 435-0540

or e-mail

info@ema.co.calhoun.al.us

http://www.calhounema.org/csepp.html#Zonal%20Map

17.

Trinity University Coates Library
One Trinity Place
San Antonio, TX 78212

Director
Diane Graves

Disaster Plan

Prepared and organized by

Laura Hayes
Kristina Howard
Deborah Nicholl

2002-2003

Disasters

Leak or Minor Flood

If risk is minor, such as a leak in the ceiling over stacks:
    a. Move library materials from path of water.
    b. Place plastic sheeting over at-risk areas.
    c. If possible, position plastic trash cans to catch water.
    d. Empty trash cans as needed.
    e. Notify Administrative Secretary of leak.
If risk is greater, such as water leaking near electrical wires:
    a. Clear area of patrons.
    b. Notify Department of Campus Safety and Physical Plant of problem.
      (or have Administrative Secretary do so)
    c. Remove library materials when safe to do so.
    d. Use trashcans to catch water, and monitor the area until leak is fixed.

2

Major Flood

EVACUATE BUILDING IMMEDIATELY

1. Stabilize the situation
    A. Call Department of Campus Safety.
    B. Notify **Disaster Recovery Coordinator (DRC)**.
    C. Keep building unoccupied until **DRC** specifies.
    D. Let emergency crews secure the building and declare it safe.
    E. **Phone Tree Coordinator** spread information and instructions.
2. **Disaster Recovery Team (DRT)**begin various duties.
    A. Contact appropriate safety and maintenance groups.
    B. **Salvage** begin gathering available supplies and contacting vendors if additional supplies or services are needed.
    C. **DRC** communicate with university officials; handle media.
    D. **Budget** and **DRC** communicate with insurance, legal.
    E. **Personnel** coordinate human resource matters, including calling volunteers if needed.
3. Persons involved in recovery meet at library or, if necessary, remote command center.
    A. Restrict Library access.
    B. Assess exterior damage; take pictures.
    C. Remind everyone of safety risks.
    D. Provide quick reminders, priority lists and inventory control forms.
    E. Enter Library, properly clothed, when deemed safe.
    F. Assess interior damage; take pictures.
4. **DRT** go over guidelines for recovery operation.
    A. **DRC** and **Budget** impart salvage plan (priorities, methods, funds, etc.)
    B. **Personnel** assign workers/volunteers as appropriate.
    C. **Security** provide building and safety information.
    D. **Inventory Control** go over inventory control procedures and designate recorder for each group.
    E. Set up command center with team lists, extra forms, supplies, phone numbers, phones, maps to keep track of library activity.
5. Begin recovery. (For detailed instructions, see **FLOOD RECOVERY** section.)
    A. **Security** set up fans, ensure light and power, maintain temperature and humidity.
    B. **Salvage** set up recovery center with supplies and workspace; go over salvage techniques with workers; contact vendors if deemed necessary by **DRC**.
    C. Send teams with supervisor, recorder and photographer to each area, beginning with first priorities.
    D. **Services** begin working on recovering records and accounting for library materials.

3

Trinity University Crisis Management Protocols

Section 1. Flood

A. Expected Impact

- Possible building content damage from flooding.
- Utility disruptions possible.
- Travel may become difficult or impossible (especially if the flooding conditions are associated with a high wind event, such as a tropical storm).
- In an extreme situation, the University may be closed for a day or two due to local transportation disruptions.
- In an extreme situation, the University may be closed for an extended period if campus flooding occurs.

B. Action Steps

1. **Seasonal Preparation (Level I):** (Upon official notification by the University.)

   ☐ Review Department Level Plans and Actions with faculty and staff.
   ☐ Review and update Library Disaster Plan.
   ☐ Have lower floors inspected for potential water entry points; seal or repair same.
   ☐ Ensure that high-value resources and materials on 1st-floor are as vertically elevated as possible.
   ☐ Have roof and atria inspected for potential water entry points; seal or repair same.

2. **Pre-Disaster (Level II):**

   1) At the Watch Point (36 hours from expected impact): (Upon official notification by the University.)

   ☐ Secure research assets (i.e., vertical relocation) and, as necessary, backup equipment required to maintain environmental controls. Special attention for:
   - Assets of high value
   - Perishable assets
   - Living organisms
   - Non-replaceable assets
   ☐ Faculty and staff secure building contents in office and work areas from lower levels of buildings vulnerable to flooding (vertical relocation).
   ☐ Contact all members of the Library Disaster Recovery Team (DRT) and advise of situation.
   ☐ Locate and secure copies of Library Disaster Plan and University Crisis Management Protocols.
   ☐ Arrange for closure of building and dismissal of staff; alter Library hours recording and web hours (if possible).
   ☐ Wherever feasible, vertically relocate Library collections, materials, and electrical equipment, or cover with plastic in areas where roof is prone to leak.

2) **At the Warning Point (24 hours from expected impact) (Level III):** (Upon official notification by the University.)

- ☐ Outdoor activities will likely be cancelled by the University.
- ☐ Faculty, staff, and non-resident students will need to be released before travel conditions become dangerous, as directed by the University President's Office.
- ☐ In an extreme situation wherein the campus is subject to flooding consider executing action steps recommended for hurricanes/windstorms (see Section 2).

3. Post Disaster

1) **Immediate Actions (to be completed within 12 hours after the event)** [1]**:** (Upon official notification by the University.)

- ☐ Departments complete initial damage assessments (see attachment A) and forward completed forms to their Vice President's office.
- ☐ Notify Disaster Recovery Coordinator (ext. XXXX) and consult Library Disaster Plan.
- ☐ Allow emergency personnel to enter and inspect building and declare it safe.
- ☐ Prevent entry by unauthorized personnel.
- ☐ Contact appropriate safety and maintenance groups and vendors (tel. nos. in Disaster Plan).
- ☐ Photograph and document all damage to collections, facilities, and building.
- ☐ Follow additional steps as indicated in Library Disaster Plan.

2) **Initial Recovery (to be completed from 12 to 48 hours after the event)** [1] **:**

- ☐ Contact external resources to obtain essential resources to restore operation, if necessary.
- ☐ Disaster Recovery Team meets to assess situation and plan further recovery tasks.
- ☐ Begin salvage procedures of any damaged property, per Disaster Plan.

3) **Campus Recovery (to be completed within 3 weeks after the event)** [1] **:**

- ☐ Alternate facilities are secured and temporary structures erected, as necessary.
- ☐ Inventory all damaged materials, facilities, and equipment, and adjust catalog for lost Library collection items as necessary.
- ☐ Initiate repair/replacement of essential resources.

4) **Campus Opening:**

- ☐ Faculty and staff return to campus.
- ☐ Students return to campus.
- ☐ Classes resume.

5) Plan Review

- ☐ Review action steps taken.
- ☐ Revise documentation and procedures.

[1] Times are approximate. Actions should be completed as quickly as possible.

> **Floods generally can be categorized into four classes – general, flash, river or coastal. The most common flooding (general and river floods) arise from excessive rainfall and/or snow melt occurs over a period of time, it usually provides sufficient warning to execute steps to protect assets and avoid loss of life. Flash floods, in particular, provide little or no warning, leaving insufficient time to take emergency actions to protect assets. Flash floods are more likely to result in loss of life.**

Section 2. Hurricane/Windstorm

A. Expected Impact

Category #1
- Some wind damage / trees down.
- Possible building content damage from flooding.
- Temporary utility disruptions likely.
- University closed for a day or two.

Category #2
- Wind damage / trees down.
- Some building content damage likely from flooding and/or high winds.
- Some minor building structure damage possible.
- Utility disruptions likely.
- University closed for two to three days.

Category #3 or higher
- Substantial wind damage / trees down.
- Building content damage likely from flooding and/or high winds.
- Some building structure damage likely.
- Extensive utility disruptions likely.
- University closed for several weeks.

> **Note: Trinity University's location is not normally considered in a Hurricane Evacuation Zone, and therefore direct impact from a hurricane is not likely to occur. However, San Antonio has experienced severe weather and tornados from Gulf Coast hurricanes, as well as extremely strong, straight line wind conditions.**

B. Action Steps

1. Pre-Disaster (Level I)

1) At the Alert Point (72 hours from expected impact): (Upon official notification by the University.)

- ☐ Review Department Level Plans and Actions with faculty and staff.
- ☐ Notify staff of impending closure.
- ☐ Notify public of impending closure via changes to telephone hours recording and web schedule.
- ☐ Identify locations of and secure copies of Library Disaster Plan and University Crisis Management Protocols.
- ☐ Follow weather advisories issued by University, news media, and local and state governments.
- ☐ If possible, quickly identify building openings and fortify same.

2) At the Watch Point (36 hours from expected impact or earlier) (Level II): (Upon official notification by the University.)

- ☐ Secure research assets and, as necessary, backup equipment required to maintain environmental controls. Special attention for:
  - Assets of high value
  - Perishable assets
  - Living organisms
  - Non-replaceable assets
- ☐ Faculty and staff secure building contents in all areas.
- ☐ Outdoor activities are cancelled, by the University.
- ☐ Essential personnel conduct final inspection of facility and review of Library Disaster Plan.
- ☐ If necessary, dismiss all non-essential staff to return to their homes.
- ☐ Finalize operational hours changes and publicize in usual media; telephone all off-campus staff to advise of closure period.
- ☐ Secure available recovery supplies; initiate phone calls to emergency response companies and vendors (see list in Library Disaster Plan).
- ☐ Disaster Recovery Team meets once more to review plans.

3) At the Warning Point (24 hours from expected impact) (Level III): (Upon official notification by the University.)

- ☐ Essential storm personnel (individuals who are to remain on campus during the storm) return to the campus. (This item would only be for specified Administrative Departments)

☐ Faculty, staff, and non-resident students are released for personal preparations, as directed by the University President's Office.

☐ All University activities are cancelled, by the University.

☐ The campus is evacuated if life threatening conditions are expected to directly impact the campus.

2. Post Disaster

1) Immediate Actions (to be completed within 12 hours after the event) [1]: (Upon official notification by the University.)

☐ Individual organizational units complete initial damage assessments and forward completed forms to their Vice President's office.

☐ (See page 8, sec 3.1)

2) Initial Recovery (to be completed from 12 to 48 hours after the event) [1] :

☐ Contact external resources to obtain essential resources to restore operation, if necessary.

☐ (See page 8, sec 3.2)

3) Campus Recovery (to be completed within 3 weeks after the event) [1] :

☐ Alternate facilities are secured and temporary structures erected, as necessary.

4) Campus Opening:

☐ Faculty and staff return to campus.

☐ Students return to campus.

☐ Student housing reopens.

☐ Classes resume.

5) Plan Review:

☐ Review action steps taken.

☐ Revise documentation and procedures.

[1] Times are approximate. Actions should be completed as quickly as possible.

EVACUATION GUIDELINES

1. Do not depend on the phone system for communication. Know your evacuation instructions and routes. The phone system can fail during a fire.

2. Close all windows and doors, but leave doors unlocked, if possible. LEAVE ALL LIGHTS ON.

3. Move as many patrons as possible through emergency exits to lessen the burden on first floor traffic.

4. Know where the flashlights are kept in your area and use them if evacuating at night, if on basement floors, or if lights have failed. Flashlights are maintained by the Fire Marshal in your area (See Appendix B).

5. Be prepared to shout to be heard over sounding alarms.

6. Walk through your area to ensure that everyone is out BUT ONLY IF SAFE TO DO SO. If smoke is present, use your own judgment about whether to make that last check. YOUR OWN SAFETY IS PARAMOUNT.

7. If you have doubts, or if someone refuses to leave the area that has been cleared, immediately notify the Emergency Personnel in charge.

8. No one should re-enter the Library for any reason until the Fire/Police Department(s) indicate that it is safe to return.

9. Keep patrons and staff away from the exits after evacuation to provide a clear path for emergency personnel.

10. Student assistants should be utilized during a fire emergency ONLY at doors to direct patrons out of the building.

11. When outside the building, go to the designated meeting area where your department safety representative will account for their personnel. **No one should leave the area until they have been instructed to do so by the department safety representative.** This will prevent unnecessary/unwarranted reports of missing staff to emergency personnel. The designated meeting area(s) for each library is:
    a) Boatwright Library: BML Front Lawn
    b) Music Library: In front of Keller Hall

EVACUATION PROCEDURES FOR INDIVIDUALS WITH DISABILITIES

During both evacuation drills and actual emergency evacuations, persons needing assistance should be helped to the nearest exit or stairwell. If the individual is unable to continue to evacuate, note the exact floor level and location where the disabled person is waiting. Exit the building immediately and notify emergency personnel of the exact location of the disabled person.

If the disabled person is unable to go to the stairwell due to smoke, fire or otherwise, the individual should stay in their office and follow these steps: remain in the office with the door closed. If possible, seal cracks and vents to prevent smoke from entering room. The department safety representative should note the exact room number and location of the individual and notify emergency personnel immediately upon exit of the premises

EMERGENCY PREPAREDNESS

Lights that have burned out in any stairways or along any emergency evacuation route should always be reported immediately for bulb replacement so that during a fire emergency, patrons will be able to exit and fire fighting personnel will have lighting in an unfamiliar building.

AREA EVACUATION ROUTES (AER)

Upper Commons (2nd Floor)

Digital Production Services Clears this area

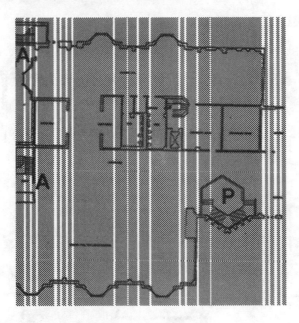

PRIMARY (P)	Down main stairwell onto first floor and out main entrance.
ALTERNATE (A)	Down stairway, through crash door, into B2 Emergency Corridor, out double doors to left. Hold crash bar down for 15 seconds and magnetic lock will release.
ALTERNATE (A)	Down stairway to exit on Gallery level (B1). Hold crash bar down for 15 seconds and magnetic lock will release.

If possible, a Designated Fire Marshall should be posted at the top center stairway and direct people to the other 3 exists listed above. This will avoid congestion, possible panic, and injury.

FIRE EXTINGUISHER LOCATIONS

a) around corner to left facing west stairway
b) left of water fountain (Microforms area)
c) left of women's rest room

AREA EVACUATION ROUTES (AER)

Bound & Current Periodicals Area – 2nd Floor

Library Systems Clears this area.

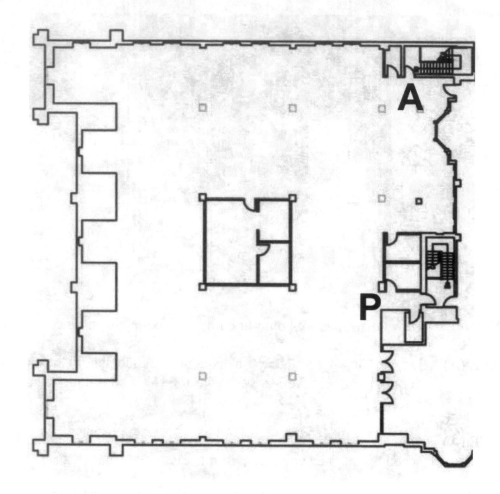

PRIMARY (P) Down stairway, through crash door, into B2 Emergency Corridor, out double doors to left.

ALTERNATE (A) Down stairway to exit on Gallery level (B1). Hold crash bar down for 15 seconds and magnetic lock will release.

FIRE EXTINGUISHER LOCATIONS

a) To the right of Current Periodicals shelving on the North side of the library

POWER FAILURE

1. Call Campus Police to advise them of the situation. Please see Appendix C for detailed information. If outage occurs during weekend or night hours, consult Appendix C. <u>Please note that Circulation Student Supervisors should check with a full-time staff member (in person or via phone) before closing the building.</u>

2. Evacuation of the library and TLC will be the responsibility of all library and TLC staff members and students who are on duty. during evening/weekend hours, please make sure the TLC staff/students are alerted.

3. During evacuation for reasons of power outage, emergency exits are NOT to be used.

4. Flashlights are available in all areas.

   a) Administrative Office
   b) Circulation
   c) Reference
   d) BDS
   e) MRC
   f) CTLT
   g) DPS
   h) Music

5. At BML, <u>ALWAYS</u>, check elevator on all floors to be sure that no one is trapped. Circulation, Reference staff, and Circulation Student Supervisors should be prepared to investigate for trapped patrons.

6. Turn computer power switches off to avoid surges that might damage equipment when the power returns. Power switches are found on the front of the CPU. When power is restored, turn power switches back on.

Appendix C

Power Failure Decision Guide
University Libraries
University of Richmond

Phone numbers:

UR police dispatcher:
Jim Rettig home:
Jim Rettig cell phone:

Considerations:

- Police dispatch or XXX often learn how long a power outage is likely to last. However they often don't know for up to an hour (or sometimes longer) after the power fails.
- When the power fails, a generator comes on almost immediately; it provides power to emergency lights, exit signs, and fire alarms. It has fuel to run for at least 24 hours.
- The BML back door and BCC card access locks from the outside during power failures.
- Some emergency lights run on batteries; these will burn for 30-90 minutes after the power fails.

Important things to remember:

- During daylight hours, public can remain in the building with the exception of B2 since it receives no natural light.
- After dark, guide public from darkened areas to areas with light, especially to the first floor. Do this before calling the police dispatcher.
- During the day on weekdays, call XXX to ask about the expected duration of the failure.
- During evenings or weekends, call the police dispatcher to ask about the expected duration of the failure. Allow time to pass (at least 30 minutes) before making this call; the dispatcher may not know anything for an hour or so after the power fails.
- Follow any and all instructions from the University Police.

Appendix F
Hostile Intruder(s) Emergency Action Plan

When a hostile person(s) is actively causing deadly harm or the imminent threat of deadly harm within a building, we recommend the following procedures be followed:

- Lock yourself in the room you are in at the time of the threatening activity.
- If communication is available, call 911.
- Don't stay in the open hall.
- Do not sound the fire alarm. A fire alarm would signal the occupants in the rooms to evacuate the building and thus place them in potential harm as they attempted to exit.
- Barricade yourself in the room with furniture or anything you can push against the door.
- Lock the window and close blinds or curtains.
- Stay away from windows.
- Turn all lights and audio equipment off.
- Try to stay calm and be as quiet as possible. If for some reason you are caught in an open area such as a hallway or lounge type area, you must decide what action to take.

1. You can try to hide, but make sure it is a well hidden space or you may be found as the intruder moves through the building looking for victims.
2. If you think you can safely make it out of the building by running, then do so. If you decide to run, do not run in a straight line. Keep any objects you can between you and the hostile person(s) while in the building. Once outside, don't run in a straight line. Use trees, vehicles or any other object to block you from view as you run. When away from the immediate area of danger, summon help any way you can and warn others.
3. If the person(s) is causing death or serious physical injury to others and you are unable to run or hide, you may choose to play dead if other victims are around you.
4. The last option you have if caught in an open area in the dorm, may be to fight back. This is dangerous, but depending on your situation, this could be your last option.
5. If you are caught by the intruder and are not going to fight back, follow their directions and don't look the intruder in the eyes.
6. Once the police arrive, obey all commands. This may involve your being handcuffed or made to put your hands in the air. This is done for safety reasons and once circumstances are evaluated by the police, they will give you further directions to follow.

University of Richmond

This Emergency Action Plan cannot cover every possible situation that might occur.

Nevertheless, it is a training tool that can reduce the number of injuries or death if put into action as soon as a situation develops. Time is a critical factor in the management of a situation of this manner.

Warning Signs

It must be stressed that if you have had contact with ANY INDIVIDUALS who display the following tendencies, that you contact the police, student affairs officials, a Psychological Services administrator or other university official in a timely manner:

- Threatens harm or talks about killing other students, faculty or staff.
- Constantly starts or participates in fights.
- Loses temper and self-control easily.
- Swears or uses vulgar language most of the time.
- Possesses or draws artwork that depicts graphic images of death or violence.
- Assaults others constantly to include immediate family members.
- Possesses weapons (firearms or edged weapons) or has a preoccupation with them.
- Becomes frustrated easily and converts frustration into uncontrollable physical violence.

"Safe" Rooms in Boatwright Memorial Library

In general:

For a *hostile intruder* incident or *unknown threat* that requires a **"seek secure shelter"** scenario keep in mind that the room should be dark and preferably not have windows. If there is a window then the blinds should be closed -- there should be minimal discernable movement that might attract attention. In addition, the room should be able to be locked and secured from the inside (hence bathrooms would not be a secure space.

For a *tornado* or other threatening inclement weather finding a safe room on the lower floors (B1 or B2) near an elevator shaft or enclosed stairwell is preferable. It is better to have fewer exterior windows and to be as close to the elevator shaft as possible. Bathrooms would serve well in this instance.

A "voice emergency notification system" alert will be sounded both on the exterior of campus and within the interior of the library to seek secure shelter will be sounded for two incidents only, an active shooter or dangerous person.
If a "voice emergency notification system" alert is heard to seek shelter then seek safe shelter, lock the front entrance doors and then monitor the doors. Only recognizably safe people should be let in carrying no articles (bags, backpacks, etc).

"Safe" Rooms from the top of Boatwright Down

TLC/ATS
Staff Offices are safe for an intruder or similar threat. In the case of inclement weather these folks should head downstairs.

MRC
The following are safe for an intruder or similar threat:
Classrooms (1, 2, 3) and viewing room (as these are all lockable and have blinds/shades)
In the case of inclement weather these folks should head downstairs.

Upper Commons & Periodicals Stacks
Administration Office
Conference Room
Small Closet in Upper Commons
Digital Production Services

Reference Commons & Reference Book Stacks
Room 171 (Business Librarian – Lit's Office)
Room 171A (Science Librarian – Melanie's Office)
Small Storage Room in Government Documents Area

Staff Area of the Main Floor
Lucretia's Office
Carol's Office
BDS Director's Office
Staff Restroom
Staff Supply Closet
(Maya and her folks should be informed that they are to join library staff in these safe rooms)

B1
Storage Room
Rare Book Ante Room
Faculty Study (Use University ZIP Code)
Staff Lounge

B2
B15 Library Staff Only (storage/dumbwaiter etc.) – next to elevator
Study Rooms B06 and B07
Digital Scholarship Lab
Single Bathroom in stacks (this one can be locked from the inside)

Albion College

ANIMALS BITES AND VICIOUS ANIMALS

IMMEDIATE ACTION

A. **CONTAIN ANIMAL -- IF SAFE TO DO SO.** If possible have the animal isolated. This could simply mean evacuating a room or floor and closing doors.

B. **CALL CAMPUS SAFETY (1234)** -- Give the following information:

1. Description of the incident including a description of the animal and its behavior.

2. Exact location (state which library building, floor, room, etc.).

3. Name of person who was bitten, if applicable.

4. Your name.

5. Name of animal's owner if known.

C. **RABIES DANGER:** There may be danger of rabies. Rabid animals may be either hyperactive or may display some sign of paralysis.

D. **ANIMAL REMOVAL SERVICE AVAILABLE:** Campus Safety upon request will send someone to remove animals. Library employees may, at their own risk remove animals that have not bitten a person. However, if the animal appears even slightly vicious or diseased, call Campus Safety for assistance. Do not attempt to remove an animal which appears dangerous.

FIRE

9/99

When a fire alarm in either building goes off, or when a fire is reported to you, follow these steps:

IMMEDIATE ACTION

A.   **KEEP CALM**

You help no one by panicking, and if you do, you may panic others. If there is a staff member in the immediate area, tell that person and let him/her take charge. Follow steps **B** through **E**.

B.   **PULL FIRE ALARM IN YOUR BUILDING**, if no alarm is ringing (for locations, see pages 6:3 - 6:12). The bells ring in the Campus Safety office, so you do **NOT** need to call that office or Albion Public Safety.

C.   **DO NOT ASSUME IT IS A FALSE ALARM.**

D.   **NOTIFY THE OTHER DESK WORKER TO SET OFF THE ALARM FOR THAT BUILDING SO BOTH BUILDINGS WILL BE EVACUATED.**

E.   **LEAVE THE BUILDING AND FOLLOW INSTRUCTIONS BELOW:**

STOCKWELL and MUDD DESK WORKERS: Wait on Cass Street for fire personnel and relay any information that you have. Go to the Quad and wait for instructions from Albion Public Safety.

MAC LAB and PC COMPUTER LAB: Tell people using computers to leave the building, then leave the building yourself.

RETURNING TO LIBRARY BUILDINGS:

If the public safety officer determines that it is a false alarm, and that it is safe for you to enter the building, return to your desk. Leave a note for the Circulation Services Coordinator that states what happened and when, (i.e., there was a false alarm at 10:30 p.m.).

Albion College

FIRE EXTINGUISHERS

A fire extinguisher is basically a storage container for a special fire extinguishing agent. Do not put the extinguisher into a fire; it may explode. Never try out the extinguisher to see if it functions. A partially used extinguisher will quickly lose pressure and become useless in a few hours.

A. LOCATION

Refer to pages 6:3 through 6:12.

B. OPERATION

Operating instructions and precautions for the use of the extinguisher are printed on the nameplate. Read and understand the instructions before a fire occurs.

Most fire extinguishers discharge their contents in 8 - 25 seconds. It is important that the extinguisher be aimed correctly at the fire before it is operated.

Stand 6 - 10 feet away from the fire and aim at the base of the flames with a side-to-side sweeping motion across the width of the fire. Move closer as the fire is extinguished. After the fire appears to be out, watch to be sure that it does not re-ignite.

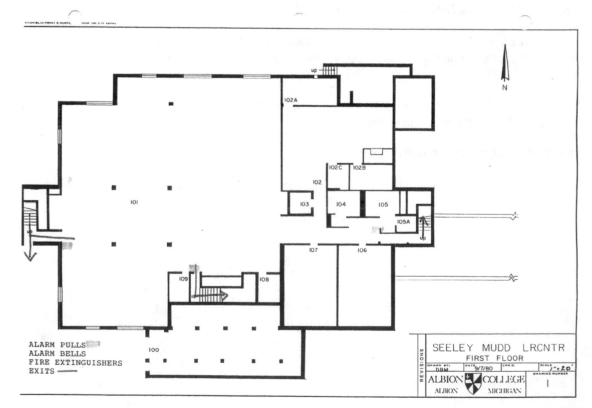

86 - Documents: Responses to Emergencies

12:1

Know the Terms

Severe Thunderstorm Watch
Severe thunderstorms are possible in the area.
Severe Thunderstorm Warning
Severe thunderstorms are occurring in the area.
Tornado Watch
Tornadoes are possible in the area.
Tornado Warning
A Tornado has been sighted or indicated by weather radar.

CAMPUS SAFETY TELEPHONE -- 1234

Albion College

TORNADO WARNING

Institute the following procedure when you receive a telephone call from **Campus Safety** informing you that a tornado *WARNING* is in effect. **A tornado warning means that a tornado has been sighted in the area.** DO NOT institute this procedure for a tornado *WATCH*.

IMMEDIATE ACTION

A.   KEEP CALM

You help no one by panicking, and if you do, you may panic others.
If there is a full time staff member in the immediate area tell that person and let him/her take charge. Then follow step B.

B.   DESK WORKER RESPONSIBILITIES

CIRCULATION DESK WORKER.

1. Institute appropriate calling procedure found in the fan-out procedure section of this manual. (Page 15:1 during the day; Page 15:2 after hours and on weekends.)

2. Post tornado warning signs found in the front pocket of this manual on main entrance and exit doors. Do not lock the outside door.

3. Put tornado warning signs found in the back pocket of this manual on the Circulation Desk.

4. Tell everyone in the Mudd building and on the bridge there is a tornado warning in effect and that the upstairs, main floor and bridge lights will be turned off (lights in the basement will be left on). They should immediately move to the Macintosh Lab on the lowest level of the building.

5. Return to the Circulation Desk. Turn off the upstairs and main floor lights. Go to the bridge and turn off those lights.

6. Call Campus Safety (1234) and report that they should call 0791 when the tornado warning is canceled. Stay near the Macintosh Lab telephone.

7. Every 30 minutes, call Campus Safety (1234) from the Macintosh Lab to ascertain current status of weather conditions.

(continued on next page)

8. When you are notified that the warning is no longer in effect, tell the patrons on the lower level that it is safe to move to the upper floors.

9. Call the Stockwell Computer Lab (0791) and tell the student in charge that it is safe to return to the upper levels.

10. Turn upper floor lights back on and take signs down.

11. Resume your station at the desk.

12. Institute appropriate fan-out procedure telling others that the warning has expired. (Page 15:1 during the day; Page 15:2 after hours and on weekends.)

STOCKWELL DESK WORKER

1. Complete your fan-out procedure calls. They are listed in the fan-out procedure section of this manual. (Page 15:1 during the day; Page 15:2 after hours and on weekends.)

2. Put tornado warning sign found in the front pocket of this manual on the Periodicals desk.

3. Take the flashlight and walk through the tiers and study areas telling everyone in Stockwell that there is a tornado warning and that they should move to the lowest level of the building, away from the windows, **immediately.** Turn off the lights in the Wendell B. Will Room, 308, the Current Periodicals Room, the President's Room and 110 as people leave.

4. Stay in the basement near the Computer Lab telephone. There is a copy of this manual near that telephone.

5. Wait for a call telling you that the warning is no longer in effect.

6. When you have been notified that the watch is over, tell patrons that it is safe to return to upper floors.

7. Turn the lights back on and remove the sign.

8. Resume your station at the desk.

9. Institute appropriate fan-out procedure telling others that the warning has expired. (Page 15:1 during the day; Page 15:2 after hours and on weekends.)

Natural Disasters: Earthquakes

Earthquakes may occur in Virginia. The danger from earthquakes is caused by what they do to man-made structures--debris falling from damaged buildings, flying glass from broken windows, fires caused by broken gas lines, and flooding due to broken water mains. There is no warning before an earthquake occurs. When one does strike, there is a loud rumbling noise which sounds like a train.
Evacuation. When an earthquake happens, the building should not be evacuated. Persons in the building should stay in the inner core of the building away from windows.
Shelter should be taken in a doorway, in a narrow corridor, or under a heavy table, desk, or bench. Exits which lead into stairways should not be used because they may have collapsed or be jammed with people. Also, be aware that after-shocks may follow for several hours or days after the earthquake. A battery-powered radio should be available so that instructions concerning the earthquake can be monitored.

For further information on evacuation, see the Evacuation Team section.

Recovery and Recovery Resources
Damage from an earthquake may include structural damage to the building, collapsed shelving, damage to equipment and furniture, water damage from broken pipes, and fire and/or smoke damage caused by broken gas lines. All damage will need to be assessed by someone in charge of building maintenance before re-entering to begin recovery operations.

For further information on Recovery, see the Recovery section.
For Sources, Experts, and Resources, see the Recovery section.

Vandalism

In the case of minor or accidental vandalism, such as writing in a book or using microfiche as a bookmark, ask the person to stop.
In the case of serious destruction of materials, furniture, etc., do not confront the individual. Instead, go to the nearest phone and call Security, extension 8999.

Rodents

If there is evidence of rodent or insect infestation, the infested material should be isolated from the rest of the collection. In the Leyburn Library, possible locations include the loading dock, and other non-carpeted rooms on campus. The type and extent of infestation should be identified. Contact the SOLINET preservation office for further instructions, (800-999-8558).

Insects

Destructive insects can sometimes be found in books or making their way through the library in search of food. The bar below each sketch is meant to indicate the actual size of the adult insect but may be somewhat distorted due to variations in individual browsers. In order to find out how to battle bugs, read *Integrated Pest Management*

Systems

All servers are housed in ITS.

ANNIE, the online library system, serves both the University and Law libraries. It was purchased from Innovative Interfaces in 1991. Annie is a "turnkey" system. We pay Innovative a yearly fee to help maintain our software and hardware. Annie contains data that our staff has input locally, which is used in the library's online catalog, circulation system, and acquisitions operations. We do "full" backups of Annie's database each day during the regular work week, following the procedures recommended by Innovative Interfaces. Backups are done using the system tape drive in Technical Services and stored there in the server room. Copies of backups are also stored off-site in the Science Librarian's office at the Telford Science Library. In the event of a disaster that were to destroy the Annie server, we would work with Innovative Interfaces to secure new hardware and restore Annie's database from our "full" backup tapes. (Contact: xxx)

ILLIAD. Vital data on Illiad includes the Microsoft SQL databases used by the Illiad ILL system, as well as the customized web interface pages. This data is backed up via automated process to a centrally-accessible directory, from which it is backed up to tape by university computing. The primary contact within UC for this is xxx, Systems Analyst. Some of the data is also backed up to an external hard drive that resides in the Technology coordinators office.
(Contact: xxx)

ACHILLES. Vital data on Achilles includes the entirety of the library website and the MySQL databases for various applications that run on the box. These are backed up via automated process to a central directory, and from there are also backed up to tape over the network. Troy has no regular backup. Everyone working on this box is expected to have their own personal backups of any work they are doing. A fuller and more detailed description of what exactly is backed up and where is available via the library system administration wiki.

(Contact: xxx)

SUMMONING MEDICAL ASSISTANCE

If someone is sick or injured and in need of emergency help, call Campus Security, ext. 5900. If the person is unconscious or unable to communicate, call 9-911, then Campus Security at ext. 5900.

Emergency Telephone Procedures:

1. Give your name

2. Give the phone number from which you are calling.

3. Give the location and any special description of how to get to the victim or emergency site

4. Describe the victim's condition as best you can...bleeding, broken bones, etc.

5. Do not hang up. Let emergency persons end the conversation. They may have questions to ask you or special information to give you about what you can do until help arrives

In an EXTREME emergency, call 9-911.

1. If the victim is a staff member, notify the senior staff member on duty.

2. Notify the Library Director (or have someone notify him/her).

3. Make sure the injured or sick person is not left alone any longer than necessary. If possible, have someone stay with the victim while you make the phone calls.

4. If appropriate, the Library Director should seek the victim's EMERGENCY CONTACT LIST to notify family/friends of the emergency.

5. If the injury is job-related, the victim's supervisor must submit a completed accident report to the Human Resources Office.

MEDICAL/HEALTH EMERGENCY PROCEDURES

Survey the scene.

1. Determine if it is safe to assist the victim(s).

2. Determine what has happened, including how many persons are involved in the incident.

a) If a victim is conscious, interview the person to determine what happened and the extent of the illness or injury.

Warren A. Hood Library   Emergency Response Manual   June 15, 2005

b) If a victim is unconscious, look for clues to determine what happened and the extent of the illness of injury. Bystanders can often give much help in this matter.

c) Look for a medical alert tag at the victim's neck, wrist or ankle for any information that can be helpful.

d) Use personal protective care when approaching the scene. For example, use protective gloves to prevent contact with any body fluids; use a pocket mask if rescue breathing becomes necessary. Both of the protective items are in or near the First Aid kit located in the emergency tool kit in the work room.

If the incident is MINOR and can be handled by the library staff: Follow first aid procedure as trained.

1. Reassure on-lookers that the situation is under control, but be ready to ask them for their help if that is necessary.

2. Do not apologize for, or accept any responsibility for, an accident.

If the incident is MAJOR (for example: broken bones, severe chest pain, person is or becomes unconscious, shortness of breath, etc.)

a) Conduct a primary survey: Check for unresponsiveness and life- threatening conditions. Check the victim's airway, breathing and circulation as per CPR/First Aid Training.

b) Call 9-911 for assistance.

i. If possible, have a bystander call for help and give the dispatcher information on what happened, where the incident occurred, the phone number, the number of victims, what help is being given to the victim and any special problems either at the scene or likely to be encountered en route by the rescue squad.

ii. If you are alone, leave the victim only long enough to call for help (with above information) and then return immediately to care for the victim. Even CPR should be delayed if you are alone. It is vital to get the advanced life support crew on the way as soon as possible.

iii. Have someone meet the ambulance if possible. This will make sure that the rescue personnel reach the right place in the building as soon as possible when they arrive.

c) While waiting for the rescue squad, continue to treat any life-threatening conditions found in the primary survey, such as no breathing, no pulse, or major bleeding.

d) If no life-threatening conditions are found, do a secondary survey: check for non life-threatening conditions that may become life-threatening of not treated right away. Interview the victim if possible, check the vital signs if trained to do this and equipment is available, and do a head-to-toe exam.

e) Remain calm. Reassure the victim, staff and bystanders. Keep the curiosity seekers away from the victim. <u>The victim's right to privacy should be protected.</u>

f) Do not move an unconscious victim except in the event that the scene becomes unsafe for the patient and the rescuer. If you do have to move someone, be sure to stabilize the neck and spine if you have ANY suspicions of an injury in this area.

g) Maintain the confidentiality of the situation except as needed to report to the rescue squad or other proper authorities.

It may be necessary to have a staff person go with the victim to the hospital. An example of this would be to help care for a minor until the parent(s), or the responsible party, can reach the hospital.

1. Offer to do any notification of family or friends for the victim.

2. Complete an incident report form if required.

EVACUATION

During the working day, the following people are responsible for each area of the library: (if Library Director is not at work, the next person on the list becomes the designated person-in-charge)

▬▬▬▬▬ - Coordination (Circulation Desk), call appropriate authorities

▬▬▬▬▬ - Work room, women's restrooms, secure register and keys

▬▬▬▬▬ – Main floor, general stacks, men's restroom

▬▬▬▬▬ – Third floor, 800-fiction stacks, heritage room

▬▬▬▬▬ – Third floor, periodical stacks, 700s, juvenile room

▬▬▬▬▬ – Lower level, barber auditorium (if necessary), restrooms

▬▬▬▬▬ – Main entrance, alert incomers

EVACUATION OF BUILDING

The building needs to be evacuated only in case of major water damage, when structural damage can be expected of in the event of major danger to occupants. The decision to evacuate should be made by the head of the library and the team will organize the evacuation. The head of the team should coordinate all activities related to the evacuation, including notification of police and/or fire departments, and supervision of other key evacuation personnel. During evacuation, elevators should not be used.

Warren A. Hood Library   Emergency Response Manual   June 15, 2005

WITNESSING A CRIME

If you spot a crime in progress, you need to be cautious when getting involved. The best way to help the police is to be a great witness. Be prepared:

1. Focus on the criminal, not the victim, during an unfolding crime. Study the person(s).
2. Pay special attention to the criminal's prominent characteristics, including gender, weight, age, height and build. (Try to use other elements in the immediate surroundings in which to base these things. For example, "He was as tall as that building sign" or "She was as wide as that car door" since most people have trouble determining height and weight.)
3. Make a mental note of the assailant's hair, forehead, eyes, nose, ears, cheeks, mouth and complexion to help the police sketch artists create an accurate drawing.

TERRORISM

HR-3162, known as the USA Patriot Act, became Public Law 107-56 in response to the events of 9/11/01. The full title of the law is: *Uniting and Strengthening America by Providing Appropriate Tools Required to Intercept and Obstruct Terrorism Act of 2001.*

The Patriot Act provides law enforcement broader boundaries when investigating information accessed and transmitted by patrons with regards to national security concerns. The law provides federal officials the authority to conduct searches of business records, including library and bookstore records, with a court order issued by a federal court, and requires that, if such a search is conducted, no one involved will divulge that the search has taken place.

The following guidelines are presented for staff to understand the proper steps to take when dealing with an agent in authority.

First Steps for the Library Director (Staff please note number 6.)

1. Identify the agent-in-charge. Ask for identification, and check it out.

For example, if an FBI agent comes in, verify his/her identity by calling the local office. The Jackson FBI office phone number is **(601) 948-5000**. Don't just call a number given to you by the agent. Get a business card for your records.

Other numbers to know:

- Belhaven President's Office: ###
- Jackson Police Department: ###
- College Attorney's Office: ###
- Jackson Mayor's Office: ###

2. Tell agent-in-charge who is in charge at the library's end.

Warren A. Hood Library   Emergency Response Manual   June 15, 2005

If the request is for local records or patron observations, it is the Library Director or designee. Kindly request (do not demand) that the agent and his/her officers direct all inquiries through the person-in-charge.

3. Ask for a copy of the search warrant and its affidavit.

A copy of the search warrant is essential, as the search must comply with its terms. The affidavit that law enforcement used to get the warrant may be helpful to you, but it may not be available.

4. Ask for a brief delay to assemble the appropriate personnel. If possible, escort the law enforcement officers to a private area.

Law enforcement has the discretion to grant this brief delay, or to execute the warrant immediately. As long as records are not in the process of being destroyed, and the library is an "innocent third party," it is likely that a brief delay will be granted. The library may be asked to "preserve evidence" while the process unfolds.

Together the library and law enforcement persons-in-charge will determine the most appropriate location to meet, i.e. the branch or the headquarters where the computer servers are located.

If law enforcement officers wait for the appropriate library personnel to arrive, it is desirable to escort them to a private area, to minimize questioning of staff and general disruption. (**You may use the Library Classroom for these purposes.**)

5. Fax the warrant to the attorney for immediate review.

If not near a fax machine, tell the attorney the time the warrant was served, which areas the warrant states are to be searched, the sorts of evidence the warrant states are to be seized, and the law enforcement agencies that are involved.

6. Staff Roles.

Staff – please stay out of the way! You must not interfere with the search. Remember that you are not required by law to answer questions from law enforcement and have the right to decline being interviewed, and have the right to an attorney if you choose to be interviewed. *There is no such thing as informal conversation or off-the-record comments with agents in these circumstances.* You are also not required to authenticate documents seized or otherwise respond to questions except as to the location of the items described in the warrant (and these inquiries should be directed to the person in-charge).

Caution on "CONSENT." If the library is asked for consent to search items beyond the scope of the warrant, decline. This includes **all staff.** The government could use any consent given as an alternative basis, in addition to the search warrant, for defending the legality of the search, e.g. to expand the search beyond the scope permitted by the search warrant.

<u>Second Steps: The Attorney Role</u>

The steps outlined here are a recommended blueprint for Library Director/Attorney discussions *before* a search warrant is served. If the library attorney is not experienced in criminal matters, it may be advisable to have a consulting criminal attorney available (even by phone).

If time is of the essence and the attorney is not yet present, the Library Director will want be as familiar as possible with these steps.

7. **The Attorney will ask to speak to the agent-in-charge or lead government attorney handling the matter (by phone if necessary).**

Emphasize that the library will do everything it can to ensure that the search proceeds smoothly, but that you would like for them to wait until you arrive (and the appropriate personnel, such as the Director/Technology Manager) to make sure that everything is in order.

8. **The Attorney will make sure the warrant is signed by a judge or magistrate.**

If there is a discrepancy, notify the agent-in-charge.

9. **The Attorney may ask for a delay long enough for the library to litigate the warrant's validity.**

This is an unusual request, but it was successfully made in the recent Colorado Supreme Court *Tattered Cover*[2] case. In that case, the "innocent third party" status of the bookstore helped the court determine that an adversarial hearing (instead of a search warrant, which does not use the adversarial process) was required before law enforcement could request bookstore records, to avoid "chilling" the public's right to read. If the library acts quickly, it may be possible to persuade the District Attorney or U.S. Attorney to direct the law enforcement officer not to execute the warrant until the library can litigate the validity of the warrant.

10. **The Attorney will examine the warrant to see if it is narrowly tailored. If not, the attorney may be able to negotiate a narrowing of terms.**

Note the exact premises to be searched, exactly what is to be seized, who issued the warrant, and any time limits for executing the warrant. Negotiation here may be possible, (such as one hour of records instead of 30 days). Targeting the specific records needed goes a long way toward protecting innocent patrons' privacy. *Make sure the search conducted does not exceed the terms of the document.*

11. **Delegate someone (other than the principal library team members) to take notes of the search. If law enforcement agents split into groups, additional staff may be needed to monitor each group.**

The monitoring staff member(s) should not do anything that may be interpreted as obstruction. Be courteous, cooperative and quiet. Sometimes searches can get chaotic. Calm monitoring and note taking can be helpful to recall what took place. Note down what questions were asked, such as where certain items can be found.

Agents sometimes number the rooms that they enter. Record the numbering scheme. Record an inventory of the type and location of all evidence seized. Your inventory will make more sense to you later than the inventory that the law enforcement officers give you. Try to observe the agents' conduct, the places searched, and the time involved in each part of the search. The agents will probably be patient with this note taking and identification process. They are not likely, however, to slow down the process or allow staff to interfere with the search in any way.

12. If law enforcement goes beyond the scope of the warrant, the attorney may ask them to desist. <u>No one should grant consent</u> to go beyond the scope of the warrant.

The attorney may call the District Attorney or U.S. Attorney to try to stop this. Do not, however, impede or obstruct. Take notes or even photos/videos if this occurs.

13. The attorney will request back up copies of all documents (photocopies) and computer disks that are seized.

Better yet, ask if you may keep the originals and turn over the photocopies. If the agent refuses you copies, record in further detail all items that are seized.

14. The attorney will get an inventory of any items that are seized.

This is important in recovering the items later. You are entitled to an inventory of all items seized. **Do not sign anything verifying the contents or accuracy.**

<u>Follow-up Steps for the Library Director or Designee</u>

15. Keep track of expenses.

In some cases the library may be able to be compensated, e.g. if the library must rent computers to replace those seized.

16. Double check to see if a gag order has been included with the court order.

You will be told if there is a gag or "sealed" order. If so, you are must comply with the terms of the order. For example, Section 215 of the Patriot Act (and other sections of the Foreign Intelligence Surveillance Act) states that "No person shall disclose to any other person (other than those persons necessary to produce the tangible things under this section) that the FBI has sought or obtained tangible things under this section." Necessary persons will include an attorney and essential staff up the chain of command, but not nonessential staff, spouses etc. Keep records of the incident in a secured location.

17. Apprise governing authority

Although it is unlikely that there will be time to apprise the governing authority before or during the search, be sure to brief them as soon as possible. They may be called by the press.

Warren A. Hood Library   Emergency Response Manual   June 15, 2005

1. Wait a moment to see if the power comes right back on.
2. If it does, check the computers. If they do not return to normal, phone the Reference Desk (x1543) or ███████████(x████)or (home███████████ If they do return to normal, leave a note for Linda.
3. If the power stays off for more than one minute, phone **Campus Safety (x1465)**. Because the phone at the Circ Desk will not work in a power failure, use the pay phone or the campus phone. The emergency lights will come on.
4. There are flashlights in all offices.
5. Use a flashlight to help people gather in the lobby.
6. Check the elevator for stranded people. When power goes off, the elevator is supposed to go to the lower level and remain open.
7. Once the power has been restored and Campus Safety gives the okay:
   -try to login the computers
   -phone███████████or ███████(work x████or home ███████████as soon as possible.
   -Campus Safety will reset all doors and the elevator. (They must reset the elevator. You can reset the fire doors with the front door key if necessary.)
8. If Campus Safety determines that the building must be closed, help people retrieve their possessions, lock up the money and leave. Campus Safety will take care of the building.
9. If there is a **power surge**, call **Campus Safety (x████**, CIT (████, and ███████████(x████Do not try to log on computers until damage has been assessed.

Power Failure

LIST OF RESPONSIBILITIES FOR EVACUATION

SECOND FLOOR: Lee Ann, Claudia, Vera

Periodicals Stacks, Study Rooms, Microform Area	Lee Ann
Third World Area, Central Area, Rest Rooms	Vera
Books Stacks, Study Rooms	Claudia

FIRST FLOOR: Rick, Tish, Amy, Thedis, Valerie, Ill new person, Kay

Gov. Docs. Area including stacks, Computer Lab, User Lounge, Business Ref.	Rick, Tish
Reference Area including stacks, Rare Books, Public Work Stations, Elevator, Rest Rooms	Thedis, Amy
Circulation Work Area, Art Gallery, Storage Rooms, Back Elevator	Valerie, Ill New Person
Adms. and CD offices and work area, staff lounge, Conference Room	Kay

Mon.-Thurs. Nights: Librarian-Second Floor; Staff & Student Assistant-First Floor
Weekends: Librarian/Staff-Second Floor; Student Assistant-First Floor

1. The assignments listed above only work with full staffing. Given the variations in our schedules due to evening work, vacations, sick leave, etc. and given that situations or drills requiring evacuation can occur at any hour of opening, all of us need to be prepared to act as back-ups for all areas.
2. In the event of bomb threat, fire, etc., **immediately call 9-911.**
3. **In a fire emergency, never use the elevator. Do not use a cell phone in a bomb threat (or gas leak) emergency.**
4. After evacuating the building, please make sure that people outside are at least 500 feet from the building.
5. After everyone is evacuated, all staff need to meet at the top of the hill at the front of the Library, to make sure all staff got out safely.
6. Assisting people with disabilities:
   Ask user with disability how best to assist them.
   - Seek volunteer to assist you.
   - If cannot evacuate physically, take person to nearest, safe exit route, e.g. top of stairwell if not smoke-filled or dangerous.
   - Immediately inform fire personnel so they can safely evacuate person with disabilities.
7. In the event of **tornadoes** or other weather-related events, guide users to the first floor staff work area. If there is insufficient time, then guide them to an area the furthest away from windows and outside doors.
8. More information is available in your copies of *Emergency Response Procedures*. For more detailed instructions, see the *Emergency Plan Manual* kept on top of file cabinets in the Administrative Office.

DOCUMENTS

PREVENTION

Prevention and Protection Measures

The Disaster Team's most important duty, and the one at which they must spend the greatest amount of time, is related to preventive and protective measures. It is imperative that a library take whatever steps are necessary and possible to prevent disaster or to reduce its effects if it should strike. Many emergencies can be prevented entirely with common sense and the willingness of all library staff to be aware of potential problems like dripping pipes, sluggish plumbing, accumulated trash, or careless workers who are unaware of the fragility of library collections.

The Disaster Team is responsible for conducting yearly internal and external surveys to check for potential problems and for making recommendations to the Library Director about how they might be addressed. Although ideal solutions should be considered, acceptable alternatives should also be presented until the ideal can be reached within a reasonable period of time. Several survey forms are included in this section. Other sample survey forms are included in the appendices. It is helpful to design or use a reporting form that not only outlines the problem and makes suggestions for what must be done to address it but also provides space to note a date of completion. Sometimes follow up calls are necessary.

The Team should understand fire and smoke detection equipment and suppression and security systems. They are expected to communicate with experts who are available to them on campus to help solve security, safety, personnel and other issues related directly to their responsibility for the preservation of the collections and equipment housed in the Library.

Disaster prevention is the primary responsibility of the Team, and they will spend the greatest amount of their effort related to assessing and implementing protective measures.

Routine Measures to Prevent Disasters

A clean and orderly environment, if not less prone to disaster, will help control and contain it.

Keep exits, aisles, corridors, and stairwells unobstructed.

Keep internal fire doors closed (in other words, leave stairwell doors closed).

Ensure that such pieces of emergency equipment as fire extinguishers and first-aid kits are accessible and in good working order. Do not, under any circumstances, place such things as furniture, book trucks, or trash receptacles in front of fire extinguishers and fire-alarm pull boxes.

Ensure that books are not shelved too tightly. This measure not only prevents damage to bindings when users pull books off the shelves, but ensures that if the books get wet and swell, they will not burst from their shelving units.

Shelve materials so that they are flush with the edge of the shelf, or so that they do not stick out over the edge of the shelf, to prevent the vertical spread of fire.

Close drawers of storage cabinets when not in use.

Store valuable materials in fire-proof and dust-proof cabinets, preferably made of steel and treated with a noncorrosive, nonstaining, and nonflammable paint.

Ensure that the trash is removed daily, especially in areas where food is present.

Fire-Prevention Checklist

Store flammable materials in a safe, cool place (out of sunlight).

Keep all containers of chemicals and solvents, such as cleaning supplies, closed when not in use to minimize the escape of flammable and toxic vapors.

Ensure that electrical appliances are operated at a safe distance from flammable materials, and that the appliances are turned off when not in use.

Use waste-paper baskets made from a nonflammable material and empty them regularly.

Ensure that the type of fire extinguisher in each given area is appropriate for the types of materials located there.

Observe the proper electrical loads of outlets and related devices.

UPKEEP CHECKLIST

DATE CHECKED

A.	Locks on doors and windows secure and keys accounted for?	9/2006
B.	Emergency numbers posted near every telephone?	9/2000
C.	Last Inspection by local fire department official?	3/2005
	Frequency of inspections	biannually
	1. Fire extinguishers updated and operable?	7/2006
	2. Smoke and/or heat detectors operable? (Ckd annually by vendor)	12/2005
	3. Water detectors operable? (Checked annually by vendor)	Self-monitoring
	4. Fire alarms operable?	4/2006
D.	Flashlights operable: (one in each dept., public desk, and Civil Defense shelter)	9/2006
E.	Portable radio operable? **Weather Radio in Circ Office**	9/2006
F.	Staff familiarized (by tour, not map) with location of thermostats, regular and fire exits, fire extinguishers, flashlights, radio, CD shelter, and where to reach members of disaster recovery team?	11/2000
G.	Last fire drill	2004
	Frequency	biannually
I.	Date of last analysis & update of insurance coverage?	4/2005
	Frequency	annually

EMERGENCY/DISASTER PREVENTION

Issues:

- o Fire Prevention:
  Building Monitoring
  Care with Extension Cords
  Fire Training

- o Computer Information:
  Proper Backup
  Off-site storage

- o Safety:
  Building Monitoring
  First Aid Training

- o Staff Preparedness:
  Fire Training
  Evacuation Drill
  Sprinkler Valve Training
  Annual Review
  First Aid Training

- o Building Maintenance:
  Electrical
  Sprinkler System
  Security System

Active steps to prevent emergencies and disasters are an important focus of Belk Library's Disaster Plan. These steps include the plans listed below.

Fire Prevention:

Library staff will assist in fire prevention in the following ways -

1) Performing a regular walk-through of the entire building to monitor for any signs of fire problems;
2) Building policy that limits all extension cords to plug banks with overload fuses and surge protectors;
3) Annual summer training and review for staff in the location of fire alarms and extinguishers and the use of fire extinguishers.

Computer Information Security:

Critical computer information will be properly backed up. Academic Computing and Campus Technology may assist in this tasks.

Safety:

Library staff will provide for the safety of our patrons in the following ways -

1) A regular walk-through of the entire building;
2) Regular building maintenance to assure working emergency systems;
3) Phone access for all student workers.

Staff Preparedness:

To prevent emergencies, library staff will be as prepared as possible in the following ways:

1) Annual fire training covering the location and use of alarms and extinguishers;
2) Annual review of library evacuation procedures;
3) Annual review of the library sprinkler system and problems procedures;
4) First aid training for as many staff members as possible.
5) Annual review of the basic library Emergency Manual, as well as including this manual in the initial training for all new staff and student workers.

Building Maintenance:

The Elon University Physical Plant will perform regular building maintenance and annual testing of fire alarm and sprinkler systems.

5. Protection

Various protective measures have been taken to safeguard Standish Library, its equipment, and the collection; it is to our advantage that the building is new (opened September, 1999), and protective features were built its design. Important protective measures are discussed below.

Location of Smoke and Fire Alarms:

Emergency exits are located on each floor of the Standish Library. Near these exits are located Fire Emergency Cabinets (FECs), each containing a multi-purpose, dry chemical fire extinguisher (see Maps of the Library in the Appendix). Staff members are not been trained in the use of these portable fire extinguishers; these extinguishers are to be used by fire department first responders. Siena has a contract with Moore Fire Equipment, who annually inspect these fire extinguishers.

Fire alarms, which are located near exits throughout the building (see Maps of the Library) are connected to our Safety and Security office in the Maintenance Building. By agreement with local fire department officials, Safety and Security will check on any alarm and, if warranted, notify the local fire department dispatcher. The Shaker Road Fire Department (Albany Shaker Road) will respond to a call.

Siena's Safety and Security conducts fire drills in selected locations (example, dormatories) on the campus, but NYS State Education Department does not mandate such drills for libraries; accordingly, no drills are scheduled for the Standish Library (see ▬▬▬▬, the Safety Officer x ▬▬▬). Emergency exits are kept clear; fire evacuation maps are posted at emergency exits and exit signs are clearly visible. Alarms sound in the library-- alerting patrons of a possible fire-- and these should never be ignored. Fire protection includes annual visits from the Town of Colonie Fire Department.

Fire Suppression System:

A delay pre-action fire suppression system is installed in the Standish Library. The fire detection and suppression system is inspected 2-3 times per year. Water detectors have not been installed. The sprinkler system is activated by heat, responding only to the affected location of the library.

Security Measures:

Security and Safety use traditional security strategies and innovative patrol and investigative technique to foster a safe environment. Safeguarding the personal safety of faculty, staff, and students, as well as protection of property on the campus are the highest priorities. The 24 hour computer lab attached to the library is protected by electronic surveillance, emergency sercurity assistance ("panic button") alarms, as well as alarmed doors. Other security measures include such standard techniques as security strips in library materials. There is only one public exit from the building, and the 3-M security system has been installed at that location. No Special Collections may circulate without special permission. Persons who request to use the library when the library is normally closed must supply a plan for providing adequate security (for example, stationing someone at the circulation desk); three persons can authorize such use: the Library Director, the VP for Academic Affairs, and the President of the college.

The Fleet Special Collections and Archives Room on the second floor are monitored when open; rules require that anyone using the room register and library staff keeps any book bags or briefcases, until the visitor is finished using the materials.

Environmental Controls

The library's HVAC must be monitored and adjusted to maintain control for temperature and humidity. A temperature log is kept at the Reference Desk, where unusually high (above 74 degrees) or low (below 65 degrees) readings are recorded. The system is set to maintain temperature in the 68-72 degree range with humidity at a minimum of 40 percent.

Humidity and temperature are monitored in the Archives on days when the archivist is on duty. The HVAC is adjusted by Plant Operations, who are notified in the event of fluctuations in either of these measures. Recall that mold can become an issue when humidity is not properly controlled. Ceiling tiles that have been damaged by moisture should be replaced, as they may hold mold spores.

Location of Supplies

Until recently, the library owned few of the supplies that would be needed during an emergency. A few basic supplies (example, mops) are stored in a closet on the lower level; the Houskeeping staff has access to these materials (see ▮▮▮▮▮▮▮▮▮▮▮— houskeeping supervisor). In early 2003 the library purchased its own supplies (example, mops, bucket, polyethylene sheeting) that would be most needed in case of water from above; these are to be stored in the L29 closet on the lower level (see 6. Disaster Supplies List for a complete list of supplies now available).

B. INSPECTION CHECKLISTS

The inspection checklists are designed to be used as part of a comprehensive disaster preparedness program. Staff can conduct periodic inspections and information-gathering activities to reduce the library's vulnerability to disaster. The information gathered will be used primarily in two ways:

- Some conditions will be found that require repair, replacement, or other maintenance activity.
- Some conditions are not easily remediable, but their existence will alert the staff to vulnerabilities that must be considered in the disaster plan.

Some of the inspections outlined here will be the duty of the Physical Plant, rather than library personnel. Work with that staff to develop a reasonable schedule for the inspections, mechanisms to verify that inspections are done on schedule, and procedures that ensure library personnel will be informed of remedial actions that are needed. Those areas not included in inspections by maintenance staff should be assigned to staff in the library. The University Librarian or the Head of Library Services should keep copies of the completed checklists and track progress in completing repairs and other actions noted on the forms.

Appendix B contains the following Inspection Checklists:

- General Preparedness

- Fire Safety

- Protection from Water Damage

- Security

- Stack Areas

Inspection Checklist: General Preparedness

General Preparedness	OK?	Needs Action (Describe)	Action Complete (Date & Initial)
Disaster plan written/updated			
Emergency Instructions posted at all staff phones			
Disaster supply kit(s) created and inventoried on schedule			

Inspection Checklist: Fire Safety

Fire Safety	OK?	Needs Action (Describe)	Action Complete (Date & Initial)
Electrical wiring in good condition			
Appliance cords in good condition			
Appliances turned off/unplugged nightly			
Regular Fire Marshall visits			
Fire Marshall visits used productively (e.g., floor plans given to Fire Department; highpriority collection areas noted; appropriate follow-up on observed Code violations)			
Detection systems …			
• appropriate type(s) present			
• wired to 24-hour monitoring station			
• tested regularly			
Appropriate extinguishers present, inspected appropriately and on schedule			
Automatic suppression system (e.g., sprinklers) present and operating			
Suppression system tested according to manufacturer's recommendations			
Fire drill conducted twice per year			
Staff trained in . . .			
• sounding alarms			
• interpreting annunciator panels			
• using extinguishers			
• closing fire doors			
• overseeing evacuation			

Inspection Checklist: Stack Areas

Stack Areas	OK?	Needs Action (Describe)	Action Complete (Date & Initial)
Shelves well braced[1]			
Shelves braced to Alabama seismic codes			
Books shelved snugly, bookends properly used			
Shelving 4-6" off floor			
No materials stored on floor			
No valuable materials in basement			
Exits unobstructed			
High-priority collections away from windows			
Collection priorities clearly marked			
Transport cases located nearby			

[1] Even in areas not subject to earthquakes, shelving should be braced to earthquake standards. Strong bracing can guard against shelving collapse and, in the event of a fire, can enable units to withstand the significant water pressure from fire hoses.

Inspection Checklist: Security

Security	OK?	Needs Action (Describe)	Action Complete (Date & Initial)
Building exterior well lighted			
Light bulbs replaced as needed			
Locks and alarms on all windows and doors			
Intrusion detectors and alarms present and monitored 24 hours per day			
Limited number of staff with master keys			
Keys collected from staff upon termination			
Effective closing procedures to ensure building is vacant			
Book drops (if any) located apart from building or in fire-resistant enclosure			

Inspection Checklist: Protection from Water Damage

Protection from Water Damage	OK?	Needs Action (Describe)	Action Complete (Date & Initial)
Appropriate dehumidifiers available			
No leakage or seepage through walls			
Valuable materials stored above ground level			
Valuable and fragile media stored in protective enclosures			

DOCUMENTS

RESOURCES (INTERNAL AND EXTERNAL)

Checklist of Emergency Supplies

Operational Supplies	Location	Quantity	Date Checked
Book trucks	On hand (library)	X	X
Boots, Rubber	Emergency-supplies closet	2 large pairs	1/3/03--applies to all date boxes that are not marked "X"
Brooms, Regular	Emergency-supplies closet	1 (others on hand)	
Brooms with squeegees	Emergency-supplies closet	1 (others on hand)	
Extension cords (50-ft., 3-wired, grounded)	Emergency-supplies closet	2 (others on hand)	
First-aid kits	Emergency-supplies closet	1 (others on hand)	
Flashlights	Emergency-supplies closet	4 (others on hand)	
Garbage bags (large)	Emergency-supplies closet	2 boxes	
Garbage cans (large, plastic; with wheels)	Emergency-supplies closet	2	
Generators, Portable	On hand (maintenance shop and local equipment-rental agencies)	X	X
Gloves, Latex	Emergency-supplies closet	1 box of 50	
Gloves, Leather	Emergency-supplies closet	4 pairs	
Goggles, Safety	Emergency-supplies closet	4 pairs	
Hard hats	Emergency-supplies closet	4	
Identification badges			
Lights, Shop	On hand (maintenance shop and local equipment-rental agencies)	X	X
Masks, Respiration	Emergency-supplies closet	1 pack of 20	
Mop buckets	On hand (library)	2	X

Plastic sheeting	Emergency-supplies closet	1 tarp-like roll (10 X100 ft.) 6 additional rolls (each 9 X 12 ft.)	
Shovels	On hand (maintenance shop)	X	X
Walkie-talkies, or cellular phones	On hand (public-safety department)	X	X
Wet-dry vacuums	On hand (maintenance shop and local equipment-rental agencies)	X	X
Packing Supplies	**Location**	**Quantity**	**Date Checked**
Boxes, Cardboard	On hand (library and local moving companies)	X	X
Bread trays or plastic buckets (for photos)		2	
Emergency Response Salvage Wheel	Emergency-supplies closet	1 copy	
Hoses, Water	On hand (maintenance shop)	X	X
Labels and dots, Adhesive	On hand (library)	X	X
Milk crates, Plastic	Emergency-supplies closet	2	
Notepads and Post-It notes	On hand (library)	X	X
Pencils, pens, and markers	On hand (library)	X	X
Plastic sheeting, Thin	Emergency-supplies closet	2 large rolls	
Scissors	Emergency-supplies closet	1 (others on hand)	
Tape, Filament	Emergency-supplies closet	6 rolls	
Wax paper	Emergency-supplies closet	2 rolls	
Drying Supplies	**Location**	**Quantity**	**Date Checked**
Clothesline, Nylon	Emergency-supplies closet	1	
Clothes pins, Plastic	Emergency-supplies closet	1 bag	

		Quantity	Date Checked
Dehumidifiers	On hand (library and local equipment-rental agency)	X	X
Fans	On hand (library, maintenance shop, and local equipment-rental agencies)	X	X
Hygrometers	On hand (library)	X	X
Newsprint, Unprinted	On hand (local newspapers, moving companies, art-supply stores)	X	X
Construction Materials	**Location**	**Quantity**	**Date Checked**
Duct tape, hammers, hand saws, ladders, nails, wood screws, plywood	On hand (maintenance shop)	X	X

This checklist was created using SOLINET's Preservation Services. A copy of the list is kept in the emergency-supplies closet.

6. Disaster Supplies List

Several supplies are important to have on hand in the event of a disaster. Some (example, mops and buckets) are considered essential in meeting immediate needs following a disaster. Others are deemed desirable; these should be available, perhaps on a shared or a rental basis.

The following is a list of the supplies in a salvage kit that is stored in the L29 closet (on the left) on the Lower Level of the library. These supplies, which are stored in a large bucket on wheels, will be used only in the event of a disaster in the library.

Polyethylene sheeting

1 roll of clear, 4 mil plastic sheeting (10 ft. X 100 ft.)

Cutters

1 breakaway knife with spare blades (recommend use of eye protection); scissors

Mops, buckets

1 24 oz. Heavy-duty mop
1 commercial mop bucket with ringer
8 plastic wastebaskets (stacked)

Flashlight

1 high impact rubber, swivel-head flashlight with batteries

Paper Towels

8 rolls of (Bounty) paper towels

Temperature/relative humidity control--

1 Hobo LCD data logger with 3 AAA batteries and 2 mounting screws
1 Hobo H8 Pro Series logger
1 Hobo Shuttle
10 Renata lithium batteries
1 BoxCar Pro 4 software (requires Windows XP Pro on host computer)
1 PC interface cable

The Disaster Team has ready access in the library to other supplies, including: **cardboard boxes, booktrucks, extension cords, and fans.**

VI. IN-HOUSE EMERGENCY EQUIPMENT:

Fire Alarms:... See Floor Plan Maps

> **Master fire alarm on main panel in basement mechanical room.**
>
> *(Any pull station in the library will activate the Master Fire Alarm and automatically connect with Life Safety and the local Fire Department.)*

Fire Extinguishers: ....See Floor Plan

	Number by type:	Wood, paper, combustible	**(Type A)**
		Gasoline & flammable liquid	**(Type B)**
		Electrical	**(Type C)**
			(Type ABC)

Heating/Cooling System:... **Controlled by Physical Plant -3xxx**

Keys: .... **Behind door in xxx's Office**
   (List on back of door)

Main Utilities:...**Basement**

> Main electrical cut-off switch: **Building transformer shut off in basement of library. Power can also be shut off from Basement Breuer (monastery) or the Palaestra.**
>
> *(In the event of a disaster requiring a power shutoff, CALL PHYSICAL PLANT/ ELECTRICAL DEPT at 3xxx - two people and special high voltage gloves are needed to throw power switches).*
>
> Main water shut-off valve: **Above stairs down into mechanical area, next to Women's Rest Room on Lower Level.**

Moisture detector ....**Basement**

VII.   IN-HOUSE EMERGENCY SUPPLIES

Clipboards (several needed) ....**Shipping Room, upper cupboard, Mezzanine**

Dust Masks   ....**Shipping Room, upper cupboard, Mezzanine**

Extension Cords (heavy duty) ....**Shipping Room, upper cupboard, Mezzanine**

Flashlights/batteries ....**Circ, Mezzanine, Reference Desk**

First Aid Kit .... **Shipping Room drawer, Mezzanine**

Legal Note Pads ....**Shipping Room, upper cupboard, Mezzanine**

Marking Pens (permanent ink) ....**Shipping Room, upper cupboard, Mezzanine**

Masking Tape ....**Shipping Room, upper cupboard, Mezzanine**

Pens, Pencils ....**Shipping Room, upper cupboard, Mezzanine**

Plastic Sheeting .... **Behind Circ Desk**

Rubber Gloves ....**Shipping Room, upper cupboard, Mezzanine**

Scissors   ....**Shipping Room, upper cupboard, Mezzanine**

Tape Recorder (blank tapes) ....**Media**

Appendix C. Local Vendors.

ITEM	SUPPLIER CO., INST., OR NAME	PHONE
Beer cases...........................	**Check Vendor List for multiple suppliers**	
Blank newsprint	**St. Cloud Times**	**259-3614**
Book trucks	**Liturgical Press**	**2213**
Cardboard boxes	**Liturgical Press** (also check Vendor List)	**2213**
CB radios	**SJU Security**	**2144**
Dehumidifiers......................	**Total Rental Center**..	**251-9332**

Dry ice	**Apperts (Hwy 10)**	**251-3200**
Drying space	**Old Gym (air conditioned)**	
Electric fans	**Custodial Services/xxx**	**2666**
Freezer or waxed paper	**Apperts (Hwy 10)**	**251-3200**
Pallets/Forklifts	**Liturgical Press**	**2222**
Paper towels	**Custodial Service/sxxx**	**2666**
Personnel (Security)	**Security**	**2144**
Plastic buckets, trash cans	**Custodial Services//xxx**	**2666**
Plastic milk crates	**Check Vendor List for multiple suppliers** to transport milk cartons	
Plastic trash bags	**Custodial Services/xxx**	**2666**
Portable generator	**Fire Department**	**2742**
Portable lighting/ Heavy duty extension cords (3-wire grounded 50ft.)	**Electricians/xxx**	**3303**
Portable folding tables	**Special Events/xxx**	**2240**
Portable pump	xxx	**3303**
Refrigerated trucks	**Check Vendor List for multiple suppliers**	
Sponges, mops, pails, brooms	**Custodial Services/xxx**	**2666**
Water hoses	**Custodial / Grounds Crew**	**2666 / 2050**
Wet Vacuum	**Custodial Services/xxx**	**2666**

APPENDIX D. – OFF CAMPUS VENDOR LIST

A.   Containers
BEER CASES

BERNICK'S PEPSI-COLA
801 Sundial Drive
Waite Park
252-6441

GLUEK SPRING BREWING CO.
219 N. Red River
Cold Spring
685-8686

CARDBOARD BOXES

GRANITE CITY MOVING & STORAGE
207 14TH Ave. E.
Sartell
252-1311

LITURGICAL PRESS
St. John's University
363-2213

MAIERS TRANSPORT & WAREHOUSING
25 McLeland Rd..
St. Cloud
251-6882

U-HAUL OF ST. CLOUD
126 Lincoln Ave. SE
St. Cloud
251-3763

PLASTIC MILK CRATES/BOXES
(1' x 1' x 1')

K-MART
40 2nd Street South
St. Cloud
251-3343

SHOPKO (West)
4161 2nd Street South
Waite Park
251-3343

TARGET
4201 West Division
St. Cloud
253-4740

WALMART
380 33rd Street
St. Cloud
259-1527

Check with local dairies:

COLD SPRING CO-OP CREAMERY
301 South 1st St.
Cold Spring
685-8651

PURITY DAIRY FOODS, INC.
427 38th Ave. N.
St. Cloud
251-0321

KEMPS CLOVER LEAF DAIRY
804 Park Ave.
Sauk Rapids
251-8362

Consultants, Services, and Supplies

Consultants

ConservationCenter for Art and Historic Artifacts (CCAHA)
264 South 23rd Street
Philadelphia, PA19104
(215) 545-0613
FAX (215) 735-9313
http://www.ccaha.org

SueKellerman

University Libraries
The PennsylvaniaStateUniversity
E506 PatteeLibrary
University Park, PA 16802-1805
(814) 863-4696
FAX (814) 865-8769

Debbie Hess Norris
Photographic Conservator
Winterthur Program
3030 OldCollege
University of Delaware
Newark, DE19716
(302) 831-2000
http://www.udel.edu

NortheastDocumentConservationCenter (NEDCC)
100 Brick Stone Square
Andover, MA01810
(978) 470-1010
FAX (978) 475-6021
http://www.nedcc.org

Charlotte Tancin
Librarian and Research Scholar
Hunt Institute for Botanical Documentation
Carnegie Mellon University
Pittsburgh, PA15213
(412) 268-7301
http://huntbot.andrew.CMU.edu/HIBD/huntinstitute.html

Bucknell University

Volute Preservation Management Associates
Pittsburgh, PA15208
(412) 243-4006
FAX (412) 361-4157

Services

Fumigation

Media Recovery

Moisture Removal/Freeze Drying Services

Munters
(800) I-CAN-DRY
(800) 422-6379

vacuum freeze drying
Building air conditioning and drying

Document Reprocessors
5611 Water St.
Middlesex, NY14507
(888) 437-9464
(888) FOR-DRYING
http://documentreprocessors.com

vacuum freeze drying

Houston Cole Library **Key Inventory List**

Floor	Key #	Location of Door	Issued To	Date	Ret'd
Basement	102303	Emergency Exit Door	Frost/8th Floor Office		
Basement	Alarm Battery	Emergency Exit Door Alarm	Frost/8th Floor Office		
Basement	PD1 S26	Maintenance Gate	▬▬▬▬▬	12/22/1997	
AV/Basement	160303	AV Entrance Door	▬▬▬▬▬	12/22/1997	
AV/Basement	160303	AV Entrance Door	▬▬▬▬▬		
AV/Basement	306303 S26	AV Classroom Door	▬▬▬▬▬	12/22/1997	
AV/Basement	100303 S26	Loading Dock Door	▬▬▬▬▬	12/22/1997	
AV/Basement	100303	Loading Dock Door	▬▬▬▬▬	9/1/1996	
Basement	160321	Library Instruction Lab	rekeyed to fit Librarians' Office Door Key		
Basement	120303	Cataloging Entrance Double Door	Lobby File		
Basement	120303	Cataloging Entrance Double Door	8th Floor Office		
Basement	106303	Receiving to Serials Door	8th Floor Office	9/20/1991	
Basement	320303	Cataloging Door from Card Cat	8th Floor Office		
Basement	320303	Cataloging Door from Card Cat	8th Floor Office		
Basement	146303	Storage Closet/North Stair	Building Services	3/19/1987	
Basement	146303	Storage Closet/North Stair	Building Services	3/19/1987	
AV/Basement	306303	AV Classroom Door	▬▬▬▬▬	2/6/1990	
AV/Basement	306303	AV Classroom Door	▬▬▬▬▬	6/12/1989	
AV/Basement	306303	AV Classroom Door	8th Floor Office		9/2/1992
Basement	120365 P12	Panel Closet	Computer Center Staff	7/22/1992	
Basement	120365 W34	Panel Closet	▬▬▬▬▬	10/1/2001	
Basement	120365	Panel Closet	▬▬▬▬▬	3/30/1988	
Basement	120365 R3	Panel Closet	▬▬▬▬▬	11/19/1991	
Basement	140169 H32	Pump Room	Lobby File		
Basement	100303 R13	Loading Dock Door	Marriott Dining	1/19/1993	
Basement	100303	Loading Dock Door	Marriott Dining		Lost

DOCUMENTS

RECOVERY, INSURANCE, REPORTS, BUSINESS RESUMPTION

Disaster Recovery Steps

The disaster recovery section contains necessary information about the techniques and methods that can be employed for recovering a variety of damaged collection materials.

For example, wet coated paper must be attended to within six hours if it is a high priority and must be saved. Film-based media must be attended to before it starts to dry or it will be lost. There are five proven ways to dry wet collection materials, but not all are appropriate under every circumstance. Team members have been educated to make those decisions.

The section contains key steps to be taken after water damage and descriptions of techniques such as air drying and vacuum freeze drying. There are instructions for the proper cleaning of contaminated materials. There are reminders to think about any related health and safety issues caused by the disaster that may affect any who are helping.

Questions are asked to remind Team members of important aspects of recovery to ensure a smooth process. What kind of work flow makes sense? Who will be in charge of long term recovery efforts.? What space will be needed and where will it be located? How does this emergency affect service to the University and what alternative plans must be made to provide needed research and teaching resources? By preparing as many answers as possible to the issues raised in this section and its related appendices, a fast and effective response and recovery can be more certain.

A Brief Guide for Successful Disaster Recovery

1. Think creatively and avoid making uninformed decisions. Make use of any planning you have undertaken.

2. Stabilize collections as soon as possible.

3. Provide as ideal an environment for all collections exposed to disaster as is possible.

4. Protect materials which have not been affected by the disaster to prevent additional damage.

5. Select the recovery method(s) best suited to the collections and to the kind of damage they have received.

6. Avoid damaging materials irreversibly in the recovery phase.

7. Reduce the effects of the disaster on the materials as much as possible.

8. Prevent any future problems which might result from the disaster or its aftermath.

Disaster Recovery Steps

    1. **Select Recovery Methods**

_____Air Dry

_____Dehumidify

_____Freeze Dry

_____Freeze Dry (thermal)

_____Vacuum freeze dry

    2. **Pack and remove damaged collections**

Where:

1. Shipping and Receiving Exit

2. Vestibule (Front Door)

    3. **Clean contaminated materials (if necessary)**

How_____

Where_____

    4. **Stabilize damaged collections (if necessary)**

_____Remove to storage

_____Freeze

_____Air Dry

_____Leave in place

Where:

1._____

2._____

5. **Record all information about materials**

_____Number of items removed

_____Number of boxes, numbered on exterior

_____Numbers of items in each box, on exterior

_____Where boxes were sent

_____Call numbers or ranges, if desired

_____Estimate of damage, if desired

_____Other_____

6. **Collect and maintain data**

7. **Initiate recovery method(s)**

_____Selecting

_____Routing

_____Receiving

_____Inspection

8. **Restore library/archival services**

9. **Repair/stabilize damaged building(s)**

Disaster Rehabilitation Steps

After a library disaster, the most time-consuming steps come once the collections are dried and ready to be returned to the shelves. They must then be sorted, cleaned, repaired, rebound, rehoused, prepared for the shelves with new security tags and shelf labels, and replacements must be ordered. Fumigation may even have been necessary. Finally, many catalog and shelf list records may need correction or notation. All plans that can be made ahead of time for how this might be accomplished and who would be involved will help provide economies of time and expense. Where will the necessary processes be carried out? What funds are available? Will library staff do this or will others be hired temporarily? Who will supervise? What expertise is required?

Any materials that have been damaged by water will require more shelf space after drying. As a result, a shift of collections and new space configurations will be required. In the best of circumstances at least 10% more shelf space will be needed. That is assuming response has been swift and decisions appropriate. If there has been a delay in stabilizing damaged collections, up to 100% more space may be required. A timely response is clearly advisable.

This section includes a list of key disaster rehabilitation steps to remind the Disaster Team of components they will need to address.

Disaster Rehabilitation Steps

1. **Develop procedures for receiving, examining, sorting collections, and locating space**

Where_____

2. **Determine necessary options**

_____Clean

_____Repair

_____Discard

_____Rebind

_____Pamphlet binding

_____Protective enclosure

_____Replace shelf labels

_____Replace security strips

_____Other_____

Where_____

3. **Train personnel**

4. **Watch for mold and treat, if necessary**

5. **Assess new space configurations**

6. **Correct database records**

7. **Return collections to shelves**

8. **Complete documentation and write final report**

Disaster-Recovery Procedures

This section documents steps to take upon re-entering the library after a disaster. It concentrates on dealing with materials--books, periodicals, microforms, and archival materials--damaged by water or fire. These materials will need to be examined as soon as the library is safe to re-enter. Steps to salvage them will need to be taken quickly. Stabilizing the library's environmental conditions--temperature and humidity--will protect its collection from the spread of damage, particularly mold.

Salvage Procedures for Water-Damaged Items

General Information

- Make an initial assessment of damage to materials based on the following questions. Begin keeping a detailed visual record (photographs, video) of the damage and the recovery process.

    1. What types of materials have been damaged?

    2. What is the nature of the damage?

    3. How extensive and severe is the damage?

- Based on the initial damage assessment, as well as the pre-determined collections priorities, decide on a salvage strategy. Severe fire damage is generally irreversible; salvage is not possible. Water-damaged materials can usually be salvaged, but the process is expensive, labor-intensive, and time-consuming. *Generally, these salvage guidelines will apply to archives and rare books, and only in rare circumstances will the staff attempt to salvage and restore parts of the general collection.*

- If damage to the collection is limited to a certain area, seal it off from the rest of the library to prevent cross-contamination. Continue monitoring environmental conditions throughout the library.

- Materials that are severely damaged should be set aside for later recording after removal from the stacks. This will allow efforts to be concentrated on materials that are undamaged or relatively easy to salvage.

- If water damage is present, take *immediate* action to lower the temperature and humidity in order to inhibit mold growth. Target temperature should be held at or below 65° and humidity brought down to 45%. Physical Plant should be notified by Dean Coburn or one of the Emergency Coordinators to adjust heat or air conditioning, set up dehumidifiers and fans, and remove standing water by mopping or wet vacuuming.

- The Dean of the Library will decide whether the building or any part of it should be closed and whether hours and services should be curtailed. If the library will be opened, then the damaged area should be roped off.

- Check frequently to make sure that measures taken to stabilize the emergency are still working. For example, is water accumulating on or dripping around the edges of plastic sheeting covering the shelves? Are ceiling tiles collecting water that will cause them to collapse?

- Salvage and removal of damaged materials is not possible without a substantial contribution of staff time. The following precautions should be observed when recruiting and training salvage volunteers, staff members, or student assistants.

  1. Salvage work involves moving full book trucks and lifting boxes as well as less strenuous tasks. Wet materials are much heavier than dry ones. Staff should be assigned to activities appropriate to their physical capabilities.

  2. Salvage work may take place in wet, dirty, and cold surroundings. Staff should be instructed to dress accordingly.

  3. Food and drink should be provided for staff, if possible. They should be encouraged to take breaks as needed rather than working to the point of exhaustion.

  4. Staff should be kept informed about the progress of the salvage effort so that they will feel assured that their efforts are worthwhile.

  - To repeat, the emphasis in the general collection is on stabilizing the building's environmental conditions and separating damaged materials from the undamaged portions of the collection.

Salvage Procedures for Fire-Damaged Items

- Evaluate extent of fire, smoke, and water damage to collections, equipment, and facilities.

  1. Note the types of materials damaged, the kinds of damage, and the extent of the damage

  2. Give priority treatment to water-damaged materials. Most damage even in a fire will be water damage. Water-damaged materials require immediate attention to prevent further deterioration and the growth of mold.

  3. Books exposed to the heat of a fire may become brittle and may require conservation treatment or replacement.

- Smoke or soot-damaged materials

1. Carefully vacuum away any loose soot or dirt.

2. Smudges on bindings, dust jackets, and pages may be removed by carefully wiping with a Staedtler Mars-Plastic eraser. Hold book or paper firmly with free hand and move eraser from center of surface toward the edge. *Never* erase from the edge in as this will wrinkle or tear the paper.

3. An alternative cleaning technique is the use of dry chemical sponges (Chem-Clene, Chem-Glide).

4. Smoke odor may be removed by vacuum-drying items in a chamber filled with another scent or with ozone.

- Charred materials

    1. The damage caused by charring is irreversible. However, if the charred materials are valuable archival documents or rare books, it may be possible to preserve or photocopy them. *Do not disturb such materials* until specialists have time to examine them and determine appropriate procedures.

Organizing Salvage Teams

A. Team Leader Guidelines

1. Familiarize yourself with the causes and effects of damage associated with the disaster, as well as the techniques available for salvage of materials.

2. Define the tasks to be accomplished and delegate individual areas of responsibility to team members. (e.g. Assign Sorters, Packers, a Recorder and a Supply Person)

3. Review the shelving areas assigned to your team and direct members to begin with items designated as top priority.

4. Indicate potential problem areas such as leather bound volumes, swollen items, materials on the floor, etc., and give instructions as appropriate.

5. Remain visible and accessible at all times and attempt to anticipate any difficulties the team might encounter.

B. Sorter Guidelines

1. Sorters must be able to remove wet books from shelving without damaging the volumes. This can be difficult at times since books swell when wet and may become wedged on the shelves.

2. The amount of water damage to an item will determine the type and urgency of

treatment needed for salvage. It is therefore important to sort materials by the degree of wetness whenever possible.

3. Using a book truck for sorting, group materials into Dry, Damp, and Wet. Assign separate trucks or shelves for each category. If using separate shelves, put dry material on the top shelf, and wet ones on the bottom. Attempt to keep books in call number order whenever possible.

4. Items bound in leather or coated paper will often stick together and should be handled and packed as a unit. Any attempt to pull these items apart will likely result in further damage.

5. Water-soaked volumes should not be squeezed to wring out excess water, as this can damage the binding structure.

6. When the book truck is full, take it to the packing area where items will be boxed. (If book trucks cannot be maneuvered in the damaged area, or if the elevators are disabled, a human chain may be needed to move items to the packing area. If conditions prevent a packing area from being established, books should be packed directly from shelves. While this minimizes the number of times a book is handled, a safeguard for items in fragile condition, it usually eliminates the possibility of wrapping the volumes in freezer paper. Even so, an attempt should be made to separate wet books from dry ones.)

C. Packer Guidelines--for Salvaging Only.

1. Wet books are very susceptible to further damage when improperly handled, but securely packed materials have a much better chance of being salvaged.

2. Packers must properly sort, wrap, and pack all items-- marking boxes clearly with labels and instructions determined by the Recorder.

3. After being sorted by the degree of wetness, books should be packed spine down in a single row until the box is comfortably full (not loose or tight). Oversized volumes are best packed flat, while business file folders should be packed vertically. (See diagram on the next page.)

4. Each volume should be wrapped or interleaved with clean newsprint, freezer paper, or waxed paper to prevent books from sticking together. If time or supplies are limited, wrapping every other book will suffice. If packing directly from the shelves, it may be impossible to wrap individual volumes.

5. When wrapping with freezer paper, place the shiny side toward the book When using waxed paper, keep the waxed side away from the book.

6. Boxes of one cubic foot (12" x 15" x 10") are recommended, as anything larger may be too heavy to move when full. Hollinger boxes or records center boxes are

ideal.

7. All boxes should be clearly marked on several sides using permanent ink, indicating the condition of the contents (Dry, Damp, or Wet), and any other instructions determined by the Recorder.

8. Boxes may weigh up to 50 lbs. when filled with wet materials. Be careful in lifting and don't hesitate to get help when boxes are too heavy for one person to move safely.

D. Recorder Guidelines

1. It is not unusual for several sites to be used in a major disaster. The goal of an effective record keeping process is to be able to retrieve any particular box of material from any location as needed to dry and, or, re-shelve.

2. The Recorder's major responsibilities are to completely document everything that happens during the response and recovery operation, and to keep track of *all materials* as they are packed and shipped off-site.

3. The Recorder will need to devise a scheme to keep track of material (call number, location, etc.) and use it consistently throughout the recovery operation.

4. When documented effectively, items should be able to be retrieved on demand and processed according to established priorities for salvage.

E. Supply Distribution Guidelines

1. The Supply Person reports directly, and is an advisor to, the Disaster Team Leader.

2. The Supply Person is responsible for obtaining, maintaining, allocating and distributing all recovery supplies.

3. During disaster response and recovery, the Supply Person coordinates the supply effort by seeing that supplies are available and distributed to team members as needed.

4. The Supply Person should make of list of supply items used so that they can be replaced.

Recovery Goals

Immediately	• Ensure safety of building. • Prevent further damage. • Retrieve records. • Salvage library materials.
Within days	• Have usable patron records • Adjust staff issues to reflect building operation changes. • Have usable collection records.
Within weeks	• Account for all library materials. • List gaps in collection. • Resume basic library activities.
Within months	• Resume all library activities. • Repair damage to building. • Fill collection gaps.

ALCUIN LIBRARY
BUSINESS RESUMPTION PLAN
Including Media Distribution

I. **Departmental Resumption Coordinator:**
Library Director with Disaster Recovery Team,
as outlined in the Library Disaster Response Plan.

II. **Priority - Critical Department Functions**

The Libraries and Media Department of the College of St. Benedict and St. John's University support the mission, values and vision of our academic and Benedictine communities by:

1. Helping users find, use and evaluate the information they need.

2. Promoting information literacy through instruction and appropriate uses of technology.

3. Collaborating with other libraries to broaden and improve access to information.

4. Collecting and providing access to information resources in all formats.

5. Providing media classroom support.

Comments:

#1 Must provide this service as soon as classes are back in session.
#2 Service will need to be available as soon as classes are back in session.
#3 Service should be provided as soon as possible after classes are back in session.
#4 If there is significant damage to Alcuin, this service will need to be moved to a different location. With the exception of receiving materials and seeing that bills are paid on time, this would have a lower priority that the first three.
#5 All auditorium-style classrooms are at SJU, so this depends on what happens to other buildings on campus. If classrooms are moved to another location, all media equipment (overheads, VCRs, DVDs, and projectors) will need to be matched to our current classroom inventory.

Priority #1 Assess damage
Strategy:
1. Contact the Head of the Emergency Recovery Coordination team,

      Security and the Physical Plant to ascertain if it is safe to go into the building.

2. The first people who enter the building need to know or be informed that they will need to do the best they can to salvage the Rare Book collections, theology collections and media collection.

3. Contact the members of the Library Disaster Recovery Team (see Appendix A) once we are able to enter the building or when we have information about the degree of damage.

4. As soon as possible, enter the building. If there are damaged materials, identify which materials can be salvaged.

5. Assess time-frame for recovery based on extent and type of damage before operations may be resumed within the facility.

6. If there is significant damage to the building where we will not be able to use it for a period of time, contact Clemens building manager to arrange space in Clemens Library for the staff to work in the interim while Alcuin Library undergoes repair.

7. Work with IT Services to make available 26 additional computers and lines for the staff to use in Clemens Library if we will not be able to use Alcuin for a considerable period of time.

Priority #2 Helping users find, use and evaluate the information they need

Strategy:

Priority #2 Promoting information literacy through instruction and appropriate uses of technology

Strategy:
1. Provide instruction as requested by faculty.
2. Contact IT Services to identify labs that are available to use for instruction.

Priority #3 Collaborating with other libraries to broaden and improve access to information

Strategy:
1. Interlibrary Loan (ILL) will be operated out of Clemens Library until Alcuin Library is accessible. We will need to inform our partner libraries that materials from Alcuin Library will not be available for a period of time. Depending on the volume of use, a second Ariel Workstation might be needed. In addition there would need to be at least one more computer for the SJU ILL staff.

2. Technical Services facilities will be operated out of Clemens Library if the building is going to be closed for a long period of time. If the building is closed for a short term, the Technical Services staff would be otherwise directed in activities.

Priority #4 Collecting and providing access to information resources in all formats

Strategy:
1. Redirect all shipments of materials to Clemens Library.
2. Provide Library 8 desks and computers at Clemens Library in the back area for Technical Services staff (the computers and lines are included in Priority 1 above).
3. Since ordering and cataloging is done electronically, all records will be available online as long as there is access to the internet.

Priority #5 Providing classroom support and instructional services

Strategy:

1. Identify how many classrooms are unavailable and what equipment was in them.

2. Coordinate with IT Services for those spaces that are projection classrooms.

3. Identify classrooms at CSB that would be available for use.

4. Work with our vendors to get equipment replaced as quickly as possible.

III.   Priority – Non-critical Services

6. Forge partnerships with faculty, administrators and staff to achieve an active role in the educational process.

7. Support the curriculum and participate in the development of new programs.

8. Serve as a locus for the discovery of diverse expressions of human culture in all areas of intellectual endeavor.

Comments

All of these can wait until needed but, depending on the situation, that could be for a number of months. As a result they will not be addressed further in this document.

IV. Resumption of Functions and Services

Minimum Personnel (This is from Alcuin Library; I am assuming the staff at Clemens Library will still be there.)

1. Director of Libraries and Media (1)
2. Library Coordinator (1)
3. Associate Directors for Media, Public Services, and Technical Services (3)
4. Collection Development Librarian (1)
5. Acquisitions Coordinator (1)
6. Systems librarian (1)
7. Reference librarian (1)

V. Alternative Personnel

For the Director, the Associate Directors as a group will make any decisions that are needed.

For the Associate Directors, the Director will back up any one of them.

The Director or any of the Senior Librarians will back up the Collection Development Librarian.

The Acquisitions Coordinator will be backed up by the Associate Director for Technical Services.

The Systems librarian will be backed up by the Associate Director of Technical Services.

There are a number of Reference Librarians at Alcuin that could serve as a reference librarian.

VI. Training

There should be sufficient staff between the two libraries to both operate Clemens Library and to run our Technical Services area without any additional training. Staff members are familiar with the Business Resumption Plan and are able to follow recovery procedures.

VII. Personnel – See Appendix B for Contact Information

VIII. Minimal supplies, data, equipment to support critical functions.

Minimum Equipment

Each person will need a desk, computer, printer, and telephone.

Strategy:
1. First week: Based on the level of damage to Alcuin Library, this group in conjunction with the Disaster Recovery Team (there is some duplicate membership) and other staff at Clemens Library will plan for what needs to be done over the next weeks and months, as well as provide service to SJU students at Clemens Library.
2. Other staff will be brought in based on need and how long Alcuin Library needs to remain closed.
3. Acquisitions and serials staff (2) will need to be brought in as soon as possible to receive material and pay bills.

All staff will need access to computers as we resume operations either at Alcuin Library, or at Clemens Library as Alcuin is being rebuilt. All of our critical records are kept electronically with the exception of the cataloging for some materials that have not been retrospectively converted. We are looking into copying these and having a back up copy as CSB. The network and access to all of our drives will be essential for us to continue work.

We will also need the normal supplies to process incoming materials. Most of these can either be borrowed from other libraries on the short term until we can order replacement supplies. We will keep a minimal set of supplies at Clemens to get us through until we can obtain more.

We will do a video inventory of the entire Alcuin facility with copies kept at:
     a. Clemens Library
     b. The Director's home.
This inventory will be updated annually during the summer.

The level of insurance has been discussed with the appropriate individuals. The amount is being reassessed at this time.

IX.   Alternative Procedures

The core to our alternative procedures is that we will be able to operate out of Clemens in the event there is a major problem at Alcuin. This will allow us to provide good service to all of our undergraduate students. We are working with the Minnesota Theological Library Association, a state seminary consortium, to be able to provide (through Interlibrary Loan) any materials that will be needed for the graduate school. This will not be easy, in that we currently do not have easy access to their catalogs, but we are working on this.

Should both libraries become inaccessible at the same time we would have great difficulty serving our students and faculty.

The library runs on computers. Should the computer network go down or should we lose power, we would not have access to many of our resources or be able to do any of our business functions. Basically without the network we cannot function. We do have the ability to access some information using phone lines, but due to speed limitations that is not a solution for any period of time. Many of us have high speed connections at home so that we would be able to do some work from home

II.   Alternative Communications

As mentioned above, almost everything that we do is over the network. We could get by without phones for a period of time, but without the network we cannot function. Our assumption is that this is true for a significant part of the University and that appropriate preparation has been made, so that we would only be without the network for a very short period of time. It is essential to our operation.

III.   Interface with other offices on campus

The main place where we interface with other offices is the Business Office. The majority of our work is with the CSB business office so there should not be a problem if the network is up and functioning.

For media, we need to interact with the registrar's office and to some extent the Special Events office.

Obviously we are an academic support area so that we interact with the entire faculty in the teaching/learning process.

XII. Alternative workplace

As mentioned above, the alternative workplace will be Clemens Library. In addition, if we find we are borrowing a lot of books from St. Cloud State, we will place a staff member there to assist with the workload. Using Clemens Library as mentioned above will require extra computers and additional network access points. We would also have to negotiate with IT Services since we share that space with them.

XIII. Valid Information

As commented on earlier, most of our files are electronic. As long as we have access to the network, we should be able to access the information we need. Our data base is backed up in Mankato by PALS staff, our network data is backed up by IT Staff and at this point in time all of our electronic materials are provided by off-campus vendors who have very elaborate disaster recovery plans.

XIV. Effect on resumption of campus business

The library is essential to our educational operation. If it is unavailable for any period of time, our students cannot do the research and studying that is essential to their education. For us to function we must have the network up and running.

Media is critical to the teaching/learning process. A very large majority of our faculty use some form of media almost daily in the classroom.

Insurance

Information on the quantity and value of library materials covered by the institution's insurance should be kept up to date. The following outline is an example of how this information can be organized.

No. of Volumes Unit Value Total Value
Book Volumes General Collections 700,000
Special Collections (insured for 1,500,000)
Microforms Microfilm
Microfiche
Microcard
Periodicals
Newspapers
Audio-Visual Materials Audio-cassettes
Video-cassettes
Music CDs
CD-ROMs
Motion Pictures not active
Print-Material
(Replacement Cost)

To calculate the replacement value of the print collection, follow directions below.
Estimate per Volume: Take from Choice Study of U.S. Book Prices.
Number of Volumes: Shelflist reading gives number of titles.
Annual Report gives number of volumes. This came to 1 title = 1.3 volumes.
The Bibliography and Encyclopedias category has been estimated at 5 volumes per title.

G. ACCOUNTING INFORMATION

This appendix describes funds available for use in disaster recovery and outlines the necessary authorizations and other procedures for using cash, credit card, and purchase orders and requisitions. Issues related to insurance coverage, amounts, and procedures are addressed in Appendix H.

Available Funds

The University has funds available for purchasing materials, services, etc. as they are needed. For more detailed information about available funds, contact the Secretary to the University Librarian.

Cash

The library does not have cash. In cases of emergency, contact the Secretary to the University Librarian to determine what can be done to immediately obtain materials, services, etc.

Credit Card

The only credit card the library has is a gas card for the Audio-Visual Departmental van. There is no credit card available to obtain materials, services, etc.

Purchase Orders and Requisitions

All requests for materials, services, etc. must be made through the proper process. This process includes creating a purchase requisition, getting the requisition approved, and having a purchase order cut. The process begins with the Secretary to the University Librarian. Persons needing materials, services, etc. should contact the Secretary to initiate a requisition. The University Librarian will then approve the requisition. If the materials, services, etc. are needed as soon as possible, the requisition should be hand delivered to the appropriate office, normally the Purchasing Department in Bibb Graves Hall. Once the purchase order is cut, the materials can be purchased or the service provider can be contacted. In cases of emergency when there is no time to obtain a purchase order, materials, services, etc. can be purchased. In these cases, a direct voucher must be entered. The Vice President of Academic and Student Affairs must approve the voucher. Contact the Secretary to the University Librarian for more specific details.

(See the attached memo from the Director of Purchasing to Budget Managers, dated November 1, 2001, for detailed information.)

Other Information

If emergencies occur at a time when the Purchasing Department is closed, generally at night, during weekends or holiday, contact the University Librarian about purchasing materials, services, etc. that are needed immediately.

Jacksonville State University

H. INSURANCE

Building and Contents
Insurance Company: State of Alabama Insurance Fund
Contact: Directory of Physical Plant
Phone: 5450

*Claims should be forwarded to the Director of the Physical Plant for processing.

Vehicle Insurance
Insurance Company: Allstate (but subject to change)
Contact: Director of Human Resources
Phone: 5007
Description: JSU does not have property and casualty insurance on its vehicles; however, liability coverage is provided for the Audio-Visual Departmental van.

*Claims should be forwarded to the Director of Human Resources for processing.

General Liability Insurance
Insurance Company: State of Alabama Board of Adjustments
Contact: Director of Human Resources
Phone: 5007
Description: JSU does not have comprehensive general liability insurance. However, anyone who suffers personal injury or loss or damage to personal property attributable to JSU may file a claim with the State of Alabama Board of Adjustments. Claim forms are available in the Human Resources Office.

[Policies are kept in the above-mentioned offices. See the following memo from the Director of Human Resources and the memo from Jerry Carpenter to State Insurance Fund Clients (dated September 11, 1998) for specific information.]

DAMAGE EVALUATION FORM

Use this form as a master; make copies of this form for use. **A separate form should be filled out for each floor affected.**

This form is to be filled out during initial damage assessment. A completed copy of this form must be sent to the University Librarian and the Head of Library Services.

1. Date:

2. Floor/Department:

3. Type of damage (water, fire, etc):

4. Type of material damaged (books, photographs, etc):

5. Extent of damage (how many volumes, reels, linear feet etc):

6. Environmental conditions (dampness, heat, etc):

7. Condition of surrounding area (wet carpets, wet walls, broken files, etc):

8. Form prepared by: _____

Jacksonville State University

POST DISASTER REPORT FORM

Use this form as a master; make copies of this form for use. A completed copy of this form must be sent to the University Librarian and the Head of Library Services.

1. Date of disaster:

2. Floor/Department:

3. Type of disaster:
   - Water (flood/leak)
   - Fire
   - Other - please describe:

4. Source of problem:
   Water:
   - Pipe(s)
   - Drain(s)
   - Sink/Toilet
   - Roof
   - Other:

   Fire:
   - Electrical
   - Waste paper
   - Other:

5. Area(s) affected:
   - East
   - West
   - North
   - South
   - Range(s) affected:

6. Approximate number of items involved:

7. Types of materials affected and amounts of each:
   - Books
   - Microforms
   - Drawings
   - Manuscripts
   - Audiovisual
   - Software
   - Other - please describe:

8. Recovery options used: (List approximate number of items treated by each method below)
   - Air Dry/Interleaving
   - Freeze
   - Replacement
   - Rebind
   - Withdrawn
   - Evidence of mold
   - Other- please specify:

9. Personnel involved:

10. Notes (use reverse if necessary):